DRESSED FOR A DANCE IN THE SNOW

DRESSED
FOR A
DANCE
IN THE
SNOW

Women's Voices from the Gulag

MONIKA ZGUSTOVA

TRANSLATED FROM THE SPANISH BY JULIE JONES

OTHER PRESS

NEW YORK

Originally published in Spanish as *Vestidas para un baile en la nieve*
in 2017 by Galaxia Gutenberg, Barcelona.
Copyright © Monika Zgustova 2017
Translation copyright © Other Press 2020

Anna Akhmatova epigraph from "Requiem" from *Complete Poems of
Anna Akhmatova*, translated by Judith Hemschemeyer, edited and introduced
by Roberta Reeder. Copyright © 1989, 1992, 1997 by Judith Hemschemeyer.
Reprinted with the permission of The Permissions Company, Inc.,
on behalf of Zephyr Press, www.zephyrpress.org.
"Garden" poem on pages 100–2 by Marina Tsvetaeva, translated
by Ilya Shambat. *The Best of Marina Tsvetayeva*, lib.ru/POEZ/
CWETAEWA/sbornik_engl.txt
"Natalia" lyrics on pages 180–81 by Gerald Moore, Roy Apps, and Shusha
Guppy. International copyright secured. All rights reserved. Used by
permission. Copyright © Asterisk Music, Stroud, England.
"Autumn," "Dawn," "Wind," and "Evil Days" on pages 255, 259, from *Doctor
Zhivago* by Boris Pasternak, translated by Richard Pevear and Larissa Volokhonsky,
translation copyright © 2010 by Richard Pevear and Larissa Volokhonsky. Used
by permission of Pantheon Books, an imprint of the Knopf Doubleday Publishing
Group, a division of Penguin Random House LLC. All rights reserved.

Production editor: *Yvonne E. Cárdenas*
Text designer: *Jennifer Daddio / Bookmark Design & Media Inc.*
*This book was set in Weiss and AT Sackers Gothic by
Alpha Design & Composition of Pittsfield, NH*

1 3 5 7 9 10 8 6 4 2

Library of Congress Cataloging-in-Publication Data

Names: Zgustová, Monika, author. | Jones, Julie, 1943- translator.
Title: Dressed for a dance in the snow / Monika Zgustova ; translated from
the Spanish by Julie Jones.
Other titles: Vestidas para un baile en la nieve. English
Description: New York : Other Press, 2020. | Includes bibliographical references.
Identifiers: LCCN 2019024829 (print) | LCCN 2019024830 (ebook) |
ISBN 9781590511770 (hardcover) | ISBN 9781590511848 (ebook)
Subjects: LCSH: Women political prisoners—Soviet Union—Biography. |
Political persecution—Soviet Union—History—Sources.
Classification: LCC HV9712.5 .Z4813 2020 (print) | LCC HV9712.5 (ebook) |
DDC 365/.45092520947—dc23
LC record available at https://lccn.loc.gov/2019024829
LC ebook record available at https://lccn.loc.gov/2019024830

FOR OLGA,

my mother, who urged me to write this book,

because she, too,

was a survivor of the totalitarianisms

of the twentieth century.

They led you away at dawn,

I followed you, like a mourner,

In the dark front room the children were crying,

By the icon shelf the candle was dying.

On your lips was the icon's chill.

The deathly sweat on your brow … Unforgettable!—

I will be like the wives of the Streltsy,

Howling under the Kremlin towers.

—ANNA AKHMATOVA, *REQUIEM*

CONTENTS

A TRIP TO MOSCOW

When the liberation movement known as the Prague Spring ended in August 1968, suppressed by Soviet tanks, and Czechoslovakia was once again under the aegis of the Soviet Union, Soviet authorities began to persecute my father, an eminent linguist, for having participated in the protests in his native Prague. It was then that my parents started to think about fleeing and settling in the US. It wasn't an easy task, because under communism it was illegal to leave the country. After a long period of deliberation in the mid-1970s, my parents went with their two teenage children—my brother and me—on a trip to India organized by the Czech state travel agency Čedok. Sixty people undertook the journey and only four of them returned to Prague. Our family was among those who absconded.

As a college student in America, my main fields of interest were Russian language, literature, and culture as well as Eastern European cultural history. I read most of the nineteenth-century Russian classics, but didn't stop there—I also researched the dissident movements in the USSR and its satellite countries. After that I taught Russian in several American universities and always encouraged discussion among my students about Russian cultural and historical issues. Later on I moved to Barcelona, where I started translating Russian and Czech literature into Spanish and Catalan. The dissidents as well as the internal and external émigré writers were at the top of my list: Marina Tsvetaeva, Anna Akhmatova, Václav Havel, Milan Kundera, Bohumil Hrabal, Josef Škvorecký . . . I feverishly translated them all. And ever since I started to write my own fiction, my novels have always dealt, one way or another, with the subject of women under totalitarianism.

In September 2008, I traveled to Moscow. Once I was there, a writer friend, Vitaly Shentalinsky, who was familiar with my interests, invited me to accompany him to a meeting of former prisoners of the Gulag. I had never met anyone who had been kept in the Gulag, but I knew that Stalin's reign is referred to as "the other Holocaust" because many more people perished during the twenty-four years of his terrifying reign (1929–1953) than died under Nazi rule (although they died over a longer period of time); most historians estimate that 30 million people were killed by Stalin's regime. I said yes.

I had imagined the ex-prisoners as lifeless shadows, but the people who showed up, most of them old and poor, were often lively. I was surprised to see many women—most of them Jews—at that literary and political gathering. While I listened to them reciting their poems and reading their stories and essays, I began to wonder how they had endured the cruel conditions of the Gulag. I decided then and there that I wouldn't leave the Russian capital without interviewing some of those survivors.

At the gathering, they introduced me to Semyon Vilensky, another ex-prisoner and, like so many others, a Jew. He kept an archive of texts in prose and verse that people had composed in the Gulag. The next day I visited him at his apartment on the outskirts of the city. "The prisoners could write almost nothing down," Vilensky explained, "because they were only allowed to write a few letters to their families every year. They usually didn't have paper or a pencil, so they had to create the poems in their minds and then memorize them. I know a few who had memorized tens of thousands of verses. They didn't forget them, and when they got out of the Gulag, they transcribed them."

It was then that I started to see the magical power of beauty—the beauty of poetry but also, as I later learned, of the natural world—for a person who has been downtrodden, and I longed to discover more about the people who had had to spend years or even decades in the forced labor camps. I decided I'd interview only women, because they were less documented than the male prisoners. Semyon Vilensky gave me a few names and telephone numbers. "These are all passionate readers, and they are fond of art and music," he told me. "In their houses you will find excellent libraries and works of art. Most of the people who survived had a certain level of culture. To put it another way: culture helped them survive."

To reach them, I had to take the metro and then trains, buses, or streetcars. There, on the outskirts of the capital, the former political prisoners greeted me with what I had come to see as Russian hospitality. Never completely rehabilitated, they remembered their years of captivity with horror, but many also told me their lives would have been incomplete without that experience.

It was hard for me to accept this. However, as the conversations continued and they showed me their photographs and books (Semyon Vilensky was right: they had all gathered impressive libraries in their modest apartments), I began to understand. What these women found in the Gulag was their hierarchy of values, at the top of which were books and invulnerable, selfless friendship.

These exiled Russian women found refuge in friendship and poetry.

Zayara Vesyolaya showed me some tiny handmade books that she'd fabricated after her punishment came to an end: the poetry that had been written in the Gulag. "Since books were forbidden, at night we recited the poems we had composed and memorized; we preferred to sleep less and to try to develop our minds through literature," she explained.

I remembered her words when, a few years later, in Paris, I visited Irina Emelyanova, the daughter of Olga Ivinskaya, Boris Pasternak's last love and the inspiration for Lara, the heroine of *Doctor Zhivago*. Irina told me that after Pasternak's death, both she and her mother were sent to the Gulag. Irina fell in love with another prisoner there, a translator of poetry, and the two communicated by hiding poems in the bricks of the wall that separated the women's and the men's camps. He left her poems he had written himself and poems by French writers that he had translated. She left him Pasternak's poetry transcribed onto minuscule scraps of paper.

Valentina Iyevleva, an actor who had spent eight years in the frozen desert of Kotlas because she was the daughter of an "enemy of the people" (her father had been shot in the 1930s), shared a memory with me. Once, after a brutal beating inflicted by the camp guards, they had to operate on her hand. In the infirmary barracks, by some miracle, she found a copy of *War and Peace*. It was the first book she had touched in years. While she recovered from the operation, she read it secretly, and, as soon as she had finished it, she started reading it all over again, avidly. Since she had no other books, she read Tolstoy's novel four times. When she left the Gulag, she filled the room she was renting with books stacked up to the ceiling. "I spent every day and every night reading; I was insatiable," Valentina confessed. "I couldn't start life over after I left the Gulag because people distrusted someone who had been a prisoner. Books gave my life meaning."

Galya Safonova is younger than the others. She was born in a Siberian Gulag in the 1940s. Since all she knew at the time were the barracks she lived in with her mother and other women, prison life was natural to her, and even today she keeps the books the women prisoners made for her. My eyes fell on one by chance: *Little Red Riding Hood*. It was made of scraps of paper of different sizes, sewed together by hand, with drawings sketched with colored pencils on each page: Little Red Riding Hood with her basket of presents, the wolf with the grandmother, the wolf in disguise with Little Red Riding Hood; the text of the story was written in ink. "Each one of those books made me happy!" Galya exclaimed. "As a little girl, they were my only cultural points of reference. I have kept them all my life. I treasure them!"

Elena Korybut-Daszkiewicz Markova, who had spent more than ten years in especially hard circumstances in the mines of Vorkuta in the treeless tundra, way beyond the Arctic Circle, showed me a book by Alexander Pushkin adorned with engravings and published in 1905: "In the camp, this book passed through hundreds, maybe even thousands, of hands. Books have their own lives, their histories and their end, just as humans do. You can't imagine what a book meant to the prisoners: it was salvation! Beauty, liberty, and civilization in the midst of total barbarity!"

There were many foreigners in the Gulag. In 2013 I took advantage of a trip to London to interview a representative of this extensive group: the Pole Janina Misik. Her family was one of the tens of thousands arrested in the part of Poland that now belongs to Belarus and sent to Siberia. They later traveled by foot across Russia to the south—Uzbekistan—to seek refuge in Persia and Israel. Finally, a boat took Janina and her family to Great Britain.

While preparing to write these pages, I read a number of nonfiction books about the Gulag, but I would like my readers to learn about it through the stories of the nine intelligent, sensitive, and strong women I had the honor of interviewing— women who, in these interviews, relived their own lives and the lives of their friends, all rich in incident and experience. Talking to "my" women, I realized that human beings are capable of great fortitude, and I also realized that there is no situation, no matter how awful, that we cannot survive.

—*Monika Zgustova, New York City, May 2019*

DRESSED FOR A DANCE IN THE SNOW

LOT'S WIFE

Zayara Vesyolaya

{1}

Zayara Vesyolaya. That's the name written on the piece of paper I'm carrying when I set off on September 14, 2008, for my first interview with a woman who had been in the Gulag. I get on the metro in downtown Moscow, at the Mayakovskaya station, near where I'm staying. I get off at almost the last stop, on the outskirts of the city, and when I come out of the subway, I feel as though I'm in a different country, one that has nothing to do with downtown Moscow. I'm surrounded by gaudy signs for stores and movie theaters as well as stands selling fruit or food from Russia's Asian republics. I'm on a wide avenue, built during Khrushchev's administration, and I feel as if I were in Russian Asia during the Communist years.

The leaves on the trees are beginning to change color, and a few are floating in the air. We are halfway into September, and I've had to put on a down jacket with a fur collar, winter jeans, and high boots. A man is coming toward me. I ask him if I'm heading in the right direction. He tells me the way. Before we say good-bye, I can't help asking if it's normal for the weather to be so cold in mid-September. "You've got it backwards: for September, the weather is pretty good this year." He smiles and shrugs his shoulders as if to apologize for the climate in his city.

I buy some white roses on the way. Later, after getting lost a time or two, I wind up at the building where Zayara lives. The apartment block is in bad shape. The lobby is filthy and smelly, and the elevator looks as though it were made of cardboard, but I do manage to get to her floor. I ring the doorbell. While I'm waiting, I wonder what to expect from someone who spent years living in a forced labor camp.

The woman who opens the door is smiling as she invites me in. She is agile and dark-skinned with salt-and-pepper hair. Along every wall there are shelves reaching all the way to the ceiling, each piled with books; interspersed here and there are prints and original paintings, all framed. Zayara introduces me to her husband, an old man with a white beard who is sitting in the living room and listening to a Schubert quartet. After a moment I recognize it as *Death and the Maiden*.

"The two of us can sit here in the study," she says, leading me into a room. I look at the paintings and drawings on the walls; there are dozens of them: still lifes, portraits, architecture, landscapes. With another big smile, she tells me, "A lot of our friends are full-time painters; these are all presents from them."

We sit at the desk facing each other, and while she serves tea from an antique porcelain pot and covers the table with plates of butter, toast, and caviar, I look at the plants on the windowsill. The geraniums, which are in flower, are arranged carefully to hide at least part of the sixth-floor view of an interminable line of buildings made from prefabricated panels. The Russians call these apartments *khrushchevki*, because they were part of Khrushchev's plan to make Moscow grow.

We start to sample the good food that Zayara has laid out on the desk, and I turn on the recorder. She suggests that, instead of interrupting, I save my questions until she has finished her story.

{2}

The celebration of Gaira's successful thesis defense was originally planned for Saturday, but for some reason I had insisted that we have it on Friday. I got my way. It's as if I knew that Saturday would be too late to celebrate anything.

"It was a Friday in 1949. My older sister, Gaira, and I bought cold cuts, cheese, sausages, lots of bread, and, of course, wine! Once we got home, we put a clean cloth on the table, where we laid out this food that we could enjoy only on special occasions (our student grants were limited), along with cups and glasses for the warm wine. Gaira decorated the table with a bouquet of birch branches whose leaves were turning a springtime green; we used an empty milk bottle for a vase. Then we stood back to take in the sight of that festive table.

"The guests began to show up one by one. Gaira and I were used to having people over. About ten years earlier, in the time of the great purges, they arrested and then shot our father, the writer Artem Vesyoly, for being an enemy of the people, and, a few years after taking him, they sent our mother to a concentration camp because she was his wife. After that, my sister and I shared a room in a *kommunalka*, a communal apartment. Since our home was right in downtown Moscow, in the Arbat area, at night it would fill up with students. We would recite poetry, mainly by Vladimir Mayakovsky (poems I knew by heart), listen to music, and dance. We served tea and toast and plain cookies. It was all we could afford, except when Minka, my best friend, who lived at home with her parents and spent her student grant as she liked, brought us something to nibble on.

"The first guests had sat down at the table. Gaira and I were preparing the wine. We poured the cheap bottle into a clean pot, added a little water and sugar, and seasoned it with cinnamon, clove, walnuts, and orange peel we had gotten from a fruit stand and dried. As it boiled, this elixir gave off an aromatic vapor. All around the table, the guests breathed in the sweet, spicy smell of the alcohol; they couldn't wait to try it.

"The celebration was wonderful. We recited poetry and danced, and no one wanted to go home, but the metro stopped running at twelve, so most of our company said good-bye just before midnight. Five people were left: my sister and me—the two hostesses—Minka, and two boys, Oleg and Dima. When we'd finished the mulled wine, we fixed sweet, strong black tea. The stragglers drank their tea and argued and laughed as though they wanted to spend the whole night talking and listening to music and dancing.

"Suddenly we heard loud knocks on the door.

"It was two-fifteen. Gaira and I looked at each other. That was the way they had come for our mother. I went out to open the door. I was escorted back by five armed policemen, with the porter and his wife following along behind.

"One of the policemen—the youngest—introduced himself: 'I am Commander Potapov.' He looked around and joked, 'Are you having an Easter celebration?'

"I wasn't amused. Who did they think we were? Did they take us for old people?

"'We're celebrating because we've passed our exams,' Gaira answered.

"'Ahh, very nice,' the commander said. 'And which one of you is Zayara Vesyolaya?'

"The commander showed me the warrant for my arrest."

{3}

That didn't surprise me too much. Gaira, on the other hand, was stunned.

"'Wait, surely you haven't come for Zayara? You must have come for me!'

"Astonished, the commander shook his head.

"'Of course, you have,' Gaira insisted. 'You've just gotten the wrong name.'

"'No! There's no mistake.' Commander Potapov made things very clear. While Gaira kept insisting that it had to be an error, he told me to find some clothes. 'Not a lot, just some underwear. What's essential. And don't forget a heavy coat and money if you have any.' He used the familiar form to address me, as if I were a child, I thought, irritated. His voice, however, showed some concern.

"One of the guests, Dima, who was as white as a sheet, started to babble that he usually didn't come to our house, he was there that day just by chance and he barely knew the girls who lived there. Gaira and I took in his words, sad for him. He seemed ridiculous. Terrified, Oleg kept quiet, but he followed what was happening with great interest. Minka emptied her change purse and gave me all the money she had. Seeing that I was looking in vain for some clothes, she hid behind the armoire and took off first a silk camisole that she was wearing under her dress and then her brand-new stockings, which were transparent and very stylish.

"'How will you get home alone, without a camisole or stockings? It's April, and the nights are still freezing,' I protested. But Minka didn't care.

"'Are you ready? Then say your good-byes,' the commander said.

"I left home dressed as if I were going to a dance. I was wearing a straight black skirt that came down to my knees, an elegant red blouse with lots of little buttons, and high heels. Two policemen went with me. The others, following the orders of the commander, stayed in the apartment to search it. I was coming down the stairs with a hand on the banister when one of the policemen crowded me so that I was against the wall. I felt like a spy in a detective film who was being taken away; the situation seemed very dramatic.

"When I got down to the street, I thought about my mother, who had been arrested two years before. After the war, my mother had worked as a nurse, and once, talking to a patient on the communal phone in our apartment, she recommended, 'Try to find some American penicillin. It works better and faster than what we have here.' One of the neighbors in the *kommunalka* heard and informed on her. All denunciations were taken at face value. They were never questioned. The whole system was based on them. She was judged guilty of being an anti-Soviet agitator and condemned to ten years in the labor camps. When they came for me, my mother had just finished the first two years of her sentence.

"A big, black car was parked outside, the so-called crow. They opened the door and put me in the middle seat. The car headed down the narrow streets of the Arbat; it crossed Manege Square, which was empty, and stopped at number 3 Dzerzhinsky Square, in front of the terrifying penitentiary known as Lubyanka."

{4}

Months later, another black 'crow' was waiting for me in the street. They opened the door and again seated me between two policemen. I was still wearing the same straight black skirt that came down to my knees, the red blouse with the little buttons, Minka's camisole and stockings, and the high heels that I had been wearing so many weeks ago to dance at our party. I didn't have anything else. The car left Butyrka Prison, where they had taken me after Lubyanka. The black crow crossed Komsomol Square at full speed.

"Once I was on the train, I tried not to see what was around me: a crowd of sighing and groaning shells of people. I made myself a promise that until we got to Novosibirsk I would only look through the barred window, and from there until we reached our destination I would only look at the roof of the train. I thought about Natasha, a pregnant woman whom I had befriended in jail: how was her pregnancy going? During the days that it took us to get to Novosibirsk, I composed my first poem:

Just look through the window!
Forget my thirst and the sad voices,
all of that now is excluded, erased:
the sun setting on the dark forests,
a field of rye with a little path cutting through the stalks.
With a red-hot iron they marked a cross,
They denied them life, they shut them in.

"From Novosibirsk, they took us on a cargo ship north to the Siberian village where we were going to work. A muscular young man with tattooed arms approached me.

"'Hey, do you know what river this is?'

"'Yes. It's the Ob.'

"'Right. And which way does it flow?'

"'North.'

"'Right. It empties into the Arctic Ocean. And it runs through the Siberian taiga, the boreal forest. And do you know what will become of us?'

"'No. I don't know.'

"'They will beat us just like they beat the landowners. Just like they beat the kulaks. They'll give us a hiding and then they'll finish us off.'

"I gasped.

"'They'll shoot us just like they shot them?'

"At that point, a thin man with hair in long, chestnut curls falling over his shoulders, and holding a violin in one hand, came up to us.

"'I'm Nikolai Biletov,' he introduced himself.

"The muscular, tattooed young man looked at him. Then he glanced at me and turned away.

"'Are you a violinist?'

"'I just play for fun. I'm a painter.'

"Nikolai told me that he had chosen to take the violin with him to Siberia instead of a winter coat. I trusted him right away because he had freed me from Mr. Muscles. I kept asking him questions. He was thirty-seven, and ever since he was a boy he had been persecuted because he was the son of a priest. He was familiar with many labor camps within the Arctic Circle. He had spent the most time—fourteen years—in the Kolyma camp.

"'Are they really going to make us get off in the middle of the taiga and beat us or even shoot us? That's what the man with the tattoos said.'

"'We'll see,' he repeated more than once, sadly. 'We'll see, but the important thing is not to give up. Do you know what King Solomon had engraved on his ring?'

"I thought about it, but nothing came to mind.

"'It was an inscription: *This too shall pass.*

"Later he brought me a handful of candy from the cafeteria. He thinks I'm a kid, I reflected bitterly. He uses the familiar form with me, and he brings me sweets. I gave him a stubborn look, and he watched me closely, not missing my expression.

"'We're definitely going up north, and there will be lots of ice and snow. But you can survive there too. I'll tell you a story about that.'

"He obviously saw me as a little girl, but I listened to him, holding my breath.

"'In Vorkuta I shared the barracks with a prisoner who belonged to the Evenks, one of the indigenous peoples of Northern Asia. One day, on the way to work (we were laying train tracks then), this man told us what had happened to his children, a son and a daughter: during a snowstorm, they got lost in the taiga. The snow, driven by the wind, blinded them, so they couldn't see where they were going. They fell into a lair where a bear was hibernating. Scared to death, the kids could hardly breathe. They were sure the hungry bear would eat them up. The bear woke up, but he didn't notice the children. He licked his paw and then fell back asleep. After a while, the starving children decided to try licking the bear's paw too. If he could do it, why couldn't they? And believe it or not, the nutrients stored on the paw filled them up. After that, they fell asleep with their heads on the animal's belly. They lived with the bear until the weather got better and they could crawl out and return home, where they regaled their parents and grandparents with the story. So you see, Zayara, we can survive one way or another. We can survive anything,' Nicolai concluded. 'Or almost anything,' he added in a lower voice.

"'Have you ever seen a shaman in Siberia?'

"'Stalin had most of them shot, but I met one in a work camp. He wasn't very young, but I've never seen anyone stronger.'

"'What could he do? Did he cure you of anything?'

"'I owe my life to him. He helped the people he liked, and he knew how to make evildoers sick.'

"'And who did he make sick?'

"'If the shaman wanted, a cruel guard might get so ill that nothing would save him. I had a chronic flu, with a fever over a hundred degrees; I was weak, sick to my stomach, throwing up and coughing, month after month. They didn't want to take me to the infirmary; they said my symptoms weren't bad enough and that the next thing they knew I'd be asking for help because I had hiccups. So Niooko, the shaman, made my fever go up to a hundred and four degrees, and then they were obliged to take me in. In the infirmary I rested for a week. I didn't have to dig for coal or deal with the dust from the mines, and I got better.'

"'Why was the shaman in the concentration camp?'

"'He didn't get along with the administrators of his kolkhoz, the local collective. Even if he had tried to get along with them, he couldn't, because he had a different way of seeing things. He knew Siberia by heart. He didn't like the way the administrators regulated everything, and they didn't like him either.'

"'What happened?'

"'One winter, when famine was devastating his hamlet, he stole a couple of animals from the kolkhoz to feed starving children. The kolkhoz found out, and there was hell to pay. The police went after him, of course, but he took off for the forest. He jumped from one felled tree to another like a squirrel while the cops sank up to their waists in the snow banks. Niooko lived for a while in the woods, but he couldn't find food in a place where there's nothing but ice and snow for six months of the year, so he finally went to the closest town and turned himself in to the police.'

"It was then that I realized how different Nikolai Biletov's experiences were from mine, from my world of books, theater, and friends in the city. I saw how that man, with his strange hair could get his bearings in any situation, and how he could defend others.

"When we reached the northern port, the truck that was supposed to pick up the prisoners didn't come, so we had to walk part of the way. When it got dark, we stretched out on the ground. Five of us slept on two of our coats and covered up with the other three. The Siberian night was so cold that our teeth chattered and nobody got much sleep.

"In the morning, Stepanida, an old nun I had met in prison in Moscow, gave Nikolai a potato cake that had just been toasted on the cinders of the fire that had provided our only warmth in the night: 'Here's your breakfast, Nikolai Leonidych. Share it. And whatever you do, don't hurt Zayara.' Nikolai swore that he could not imagine doing anything bad to me. As he said it, he stammered a little, and I noticed that he had also blushed."

{5}

After a little while, a number of trucks pulled up. The road was rough, and we bumped into one another constantly. Just as I'd done on the train, I looked through the window or at the roof. Again, I concentrated on the beauty of what I saw around us. A plain, covered with grass and the occasional stand of rickety birch trees. Someone behind me said that the Vasyugan Swamp was nearby.

"'It won't be so awful,' the old country people just behind me were saying, 'we'll be stuck with forced labor, but they aren't taking us to a concentration camp. Deportation isn't like the camps. Have you ever been in one?'

"'Yes, north of Kotlas.'

"'I was in Kolyma. Deportation is nothing compared with the work camps north of the Arctic Circle.'

"'But wait until they send you to the kolkhoz, and they don't pay you for your work. You'll die of hunger just like a mangy dog. In the camps, at least they feed you.'

"'What are you talking about! There's nothing worse in the world than a camp. You can always find something to eat. The main thing is don't get shut up in a camp!'

"Other voices joined the conversation. Most agreed that any kind of deportation was better than a camp. The old man who had served a sentence in Kotlas explained how they punished people who didn't follow the rules: they took off all their clothes, tied them to a tree, and left them all night in the taiga so that a cloud of mosquitoes and enormous Siberian flies ate them alive. The man who'd been in Kolyma said that they did the same thing there in the summer and in the winter they left people naked in the snow, and with the temperature at fifty below, they hosed them down. Nobody survived. I couldn't believe what I was hearing.

"'In our Soviet camps? To our Russian people? That can't be!'

"The old man looked at me for a minute, made a face and didn't answer. I understood that what he was saying was true. A different, younger man changed the subject: 'Why did they deport you?'

"'Because of my father; he's an enemy of the people.'

"'Ahh . . . but Stalin said that the child should not be blamed for what the father has done. Write Stalin. He'll let you out, for sure.'

"'Do you think so?'

"'You have to write him. This is a misunderstanding. You'll see as soon as Stalin finds out. Will you write him?'

"'I will.'

"The first little villages were coming into view: ramshackle cabins made of wood, or actually of tree trunks, with holes in the roofs, the fences collapsed, and—wherever you looked—the streets covered in mud."

{6}

As soon as we reached our destination, the village of Pikhtovka, I found the post office and sent a note to my mother:

> *Don't worry, Mama. Gaira and I are fine. They arrested me*
> *first and then Gaira. They told me about her in the interro-*
> *gations. We haven't written you for so long because we were*
> *in prison, but now that we've come out I'll write regularly.*
> *We're not exactly free, far from it. We've been deported for five*
> *years, Gaira to Kazakhstan and me to Siberia. I don't know*
> *my address yet, but as soon as I do, I'll send it to you. I'm in*
> *Pikhtovka, a little village. It's called that because it's surrounded*
> *by forests of pikhtas, Siberian fir trees.*
>
> *Kisses,*
> *Zayara*

"I stretched out on the floor of the local schoolhouse, which was empty for summer vacation. I couldn't sleep. I thought about my friend Natasha from the Moscow prison. She had been so kind and helpful and I really missed her. Natasha had been expecting a baby, but they had still shut her in prison and were as hard on her as they were on the rest of us. When they transferred me to the work camp, another inmate had slipped tiny, folded-up scraps of paper into my hand: a letter from Natasha. During all the time we had been together, I had insisted that whoever left first should write to the other, telling her everything that had happened. After all my entreaties, Natasha, who had been the first to leave, had written me this letter in microscopic handwriting. I had managed to sneak it through all the security checks. I had been afraid to read it before, on the train and the boat, but now in the school by myself, I tried to read it by the light of a lantern. The light just wasn't strong enough, and I gave up.

"The next day I went to get my work assignment.

"'I'm a painter, and I need a helper,' Nikolai said, putting his arm around my shoulders. I realized then that I was still wearing the clothes I'd put on for the party in Moscow the day they arrested me: my black skirt, the elegant red blouse, and the high heels. The man who was passing out the work assignments looked sideways at us, at Nikolai and me, as if we were suspicious characters.

"Then he said, 'Leaving the village is forbidden. You'd be runaways.'

"'How about the forest?' I asked him.

"'What about the forest?'

"'Can we take a walk in the forest?'

"'Not really, just as far as the tree line.'

"That evening, at twilight, we set off to find a place to stay. Nobody wanted to take us in, and finally somebody suggested that we ask separately, because we looked like a young couple who'd want to have a child, and that made people think twice about letting us stay. I had the idea of asking at the post office. They gave me a place there, but the first night a piece of the roof crashed down; luckily it missed me.

"The next day I set off to dig; that was the work I'd been assigned. They figured Nikolai's proposal about a painter and his helper was a joke. I took hold of the pick and the pail and started digging and putting the dirt aside with great enthusiasm, but after a few hours, my hands began to bleed. At the end of my feverish day of work, I went to get my pay.

"'You haven't filled half your quota. The way you're going you won't earn enough to eat,' the guy in charge told me sadly, and he put a miserable pair of kopeks in my hand.

"I went home and stretched out on the floor. I didn't have it in me to sweep out the brick and the plaster that had fallen. I was so tired that I couldn't even get up; I couldn't move. I just lay on the floor, and for the first time since I had been arrested, I started crying."

{7}

In the morning, before dawn, Nikolai brought me breakfast. When we had eaten, chatted, and drunk our hot tea, two glasses each, I talked to him about Natasha. Nikolai asked me a lot of questions. Then I asked him to read Natasha's letter out loud. I had a feeling that it would be a confession of some sort, and I wanted to have somebody with me.

On a warm morning in July 1949, we were sitting on the edge of the station platform, our feet dangling over the tracks. There were two of us: a young soldier armed with a machine gun (the other guard had gone for hot water) and me, who until just before that summer had been a graduate student at the Moscow City University. I was twenty-seven years old, eight months pregnant, and condemned to five years of exile in the Kokchetav area.

As soon as the other guard had gone, the young one asked me in a low voice, "What have you done? What are you guilty of?"

"I'm not guilty of anything."

I didn't feel like talking. I was worn out and worried. For a few days, as far as I could tell my baby hadn't been moving at all. The day before, during a check-up they'd performed in jail, I had realized that things were not going well when I saw the expressions on the faces of the doctors who examined me. I was even more alarmed when I heard some of what they were saying. I had hoped that they'd take me out of the shared cell and put me in the prison hospital in Butyrka until I had the baby, but the next day they hurriedly dispatched me to Kazakhstan. They were in such a rush to get rid of me that they didn't even wait until they had a group going to the same place: they put me in an empty train car, with an escort of two guards, and that's how I reached the station where I was sitting on the platform. We were waiting for another train with a group of prisoners headed in the same direction.

"But I'd really like to know: Why are you a prisoner?" the guard insisted, looking around to make sure nobody could hear him.

"It's a very long story...."

Finally, I told him. "In 1937 they arrested my stepfather and sent him to a concentration camp. He had raised me. Later, one of our neighbors, who wanted one of the rooms we lived in for herself, denounced my mother. They arrested her on New Year's Eve.

"Later they were going to send my little brother, Felix, and me to an orphanage, but the director of our school, Klavdia Vasilyevna Poltavskaya, put a stop to that. Thanks to her help, our grandfather, who was eighty, was given a small pension and money for our schooling. Klavdia Vasilyevna found students so that I, along with other kids who had lost their parents, could give them private classes. That's how, when I was fourteen, I started teaching. My earnings only gave me enough money to pay for breakfast at school and buy teaching manuals and note-books. We didn't have enough to eat, so I began to suffer from tuberculosis. My mother's friends helped us: Ludmila Ivanovna Krasavina and Tatiana Vasilyevna Almasova, whose husbands had both been shot. The mothers of our school friends also provided us with a bit to eat.

"I was a first-year student at the City University of Moscow when, on October 16, 1941, I volunteered to go to the front—I had just finished a course in nursing—and I became a fighter in the Third Communist Division from Moscow. At that point, my brother Felix worked at one of the arms factories in the capital.

"In 1942, I was injured in battle; they demobilized me, and I returned to Moscow, where right away I started to work as a nurse in a hospital. At the same time, I studied at the School of History, since classes were free then. I repeatedly asked to go back to the front, but as soon as I turned in the form, they would find some reason to reject it.

"In 1948, when they started to arrest and deport the wives of condemned men all over again, their children, grown up now, were also at risk. They arrested Felix first, and then me, in 1949."

While I was talking, the second guard had come back with hot water. The young soldier gave it to me, along with a piece of bread and a little cheese.

"Take this; eat something."

"Thank you, but I don't need it. We only left Moscow a day ago."

It was hard to believe that it had only been a day since I was walking along the secondary tracks at the Kazan station in Moscow, accompanied by two soldiers who, considering my pregnant state, were grappling with my bags, a cardboard suitcase, and a sack made out of mattress ticking, filled to overflowing with baby clothes, diapers, cans of condensed milk, and sugar. My husband had provided me with all this after the end of my legal proceedings, which had lasted four months. Until it was over, the judge had forbidden me to receive packages and money from outside. In the cell, you, Zayara, my new friend, gave me food.

While we waited for the train in that station out in the provinces, I remembered the clock in the tower at the Kazan station, which had tolled my departure on so many of my trips: to the dacha when I was a child and, just after the war, to the concentration camp to see my mother. The section of the camp where she was serving her sentence was called Zhanaarka, so I associated it with Joan of Arc, who interested me because I wanted to be a historian. As it had in the past, the train left the station at Kazan and took me far away from Moscow. They sentenced me to deportation according to sections 10 and 12 in article 58 of the penal code, which condemned the crimes of "anti-Soviet propaganda" and "failure to denounce." I certainly had no anti-Soviet feelings, but, in reference to section 12, it's true that I did not denounce my own brother. Earlier in 1948, in Astrakhan, where Felix was receiving occupational training, some of the students who were interested in literature, including my brother, would get together from time to time to read the poems and short stories that they all wrote. Soon that literary cenacle had become a young persons' association called Leninist Free Thought. Things took their usual course: a provocateur, a group trial, all found guilty, and a sentence of ten years for each one.

But, before all that happened, Felix had sent me a letter in which he talked about his literary group. When I realized that those young men weren't just discussing literature, I wrote back to my brother warning him to be more careful. But it was too late: Felix was already in prison. My letter was intercepted, and it served as proof to incriminate me. Apart from accusing me of knowing about my brother's "criminal" activity and not denouncing him, I was guilty of sympathizing with his ideas.

"You have the same ideas as your brother and his accomplices. That's why you warned him. And you were right. They had become an anti-Soviet organization, and that's what I'm going to put down in the interrogation report."

"It's not true!" I shouted at the examining magistrate.

I got up from my chair. The magistrate made me stand up so long that I fainted and fell on the floor. He gave me some ammonia to smell, and I regained consciousness.

"Get up!"

The interrogation had started at about ten that night. When the magistrate called the guard and told him to take me back to my cell, it was already dawn. Another form of torture awaited me in the cell. During the day, prisoners were forbidden to lie down for even a minute. The man in charge of guarding them kept his eye to the peephole. Would night never come? They finally announced bedtime. I lay down but had barely closed my eyes when the jailer opened the heavy door with a clang and called me to another interrogation. I got dressed, but I had a hard time getting my shoes on, because my feet were swollen. One interrogation followed another, night after night, with insults, warnings, and the cry of "Get up!" that I still hear in my nightmares.

"I won't sign, I won't sign!" I kept on saying, taking a firm stand, whenever the magistrate shoved the interrogation report that he had made up himself in front of me.

When I was in the cell, I wondered about things that seemed, at first, easy to answer: Why did they leave the blinding light on all night long? Why did the interrogations almost always take place at night? Why did we have to use a bucket to do our business when the prison was an old hotel with parquet floors and running water? Why did they yank all the buttons and hooks and eyes off our clothes and even take the elastic out of our underwear? In any event, we took care of the button problem by making our own buttons out of morsels of bread and created garters for our stockings by cutting off the hems of our skirts. Those "garters" held up our stockings so well that they almost never fell off.

I finally realized that the whole objective of the prison routine was to humiliate us and to break our spirits.

My guards were worn out by the heat, and they looked impatiently for the train. I was even more impatient than they were, because in my condition I needed to get where I was going as soon as possible.

I stayed for three weeks at the Kuybyshev prison, which was a junction for groups of detainees who were destined for other camps and jails. Right away, they gave me a lower bunk, near the window, but I still felt as though I couldn't breathe. I'd walk for hours in the narrow passageway between the lines of bunks, hoping this would help my baby. The baby still hadn't moved, but my naïvete kept me from realizing just what that meant. More than once I remembered, in detail, how I had been transferred from Butyrka Prison to the hospital for a medical check-up, and then how they had rushed me back to Lubyanka Prison so fast that it made me suspicious. A woman doctor at Lubyanka had written I don't know what on a sheet of paper, and before I knew it they had me in a police van packed with people. Looking through a barred window, I had seen the familiar contours of Novoslobodskaya Street, Kurnikov's house, the pastry shop, and finally the corner where Palikha house, my own house, stood.

"There's my house!" I couldn't help shouting.

"And mine!" said the girl, who was sitting next to me.

It turned out that she was my namesake. Just like my brother and me, the Gesiter sisters, Natasha and Inna, had lived without their parents since 1937, and, like us, they had ended up in jail.

There were so many things I obsessed about during those weeks I spent waiting in Kuybyshev Prison. I could imagine how worried my husband would be about me and our future baby. After what had happened to Felix, Mama must have been twice as worried about me because I had been arrested. After finishing her time and losing the right to live in one of the big cities, my mother was working in a fish factory in the Astrakhan area.

I thought, too, about my stepfather, who had died in a camp. Pavel Fyodorovich Dorofeev, the commander of a mounted division and later an important official in the Party, married my mother when I was ten. I remember our first meeting at the house on the wharf where my mother took me. I was impressed by the sober atmosphere of his bachelor's quarters. The only decoration was a firearm with his name engraved on it, a present and a kind of tribute, from the commander of the Kovtiukh brigade. My stepfather had accompanied him on the Taman expedition. This needs an explanation.

One day in the summer of 1937 we were with Pavel in one of the vacation homes provided for cadres of the Party. Over lunch, his friend Piotr Ivanovich Smorodin, second secretary of the regional committee of Leningrad and ex-secretary general of the Central Committee of Young Communists in Russia, began to address the gathering: "Don't you realize it's time to stop and think about what's happening in this country? We have to do something! If we don't, they'll fall on us all as if we were hens in a henhouse!" At first the guests were taken aback; then they all left the table as fast as they could, except for Pavel, who stayed with Smorodin.

The final part of the trip, from Kokchetav to Volodarovka, a regional center, was the shortest. They shoved us onto the bed of a truck. One of the guards climbed up into the cabin. A heavy chain separated the prisoners from our guards. Despite

*everything I tried to do to stop it, every time the truck hit a
pothole, my stomach hit the chain.*

*After about fifty kilometers, the truck stopped to pick up a
man who climbed in the back with us. He was wearing a work
jacket lined with cotton and he looked like one of the intelligentsia. He turned out to be a deported schoolmaster.*

*"Aren't you ashamed?" he demanded in a Polish accent.
"The guy rides in the cab, and this poor woman. . . . She's probably going to give birth before we get there!"*

It was only then that they moved me to the cabin.

*When we'd just gotten to Volodarovka, I started to have
contractions. Even though there were a number of vehicles in
the Regional Ministry of Internal Affairs, I was forced to walk
to the hospital. Vladimir Ivanovich Lebedev, a journalist from
Moscow whom I'd met on the trip, almost had to carry me
across that huge town.*

In the Volodarovka hospital, I gave birth to a dead baby. . . .

"I fell to the floor and covered my head with my overcoat.
Nikolai put his hand on my shoulder and, until it was time to
set off for work, he played music for me. He put all his emotion into the Allegro molto appassionato from Felix Mendelssohn's *Violin Concerto.*"

{8}

Nikolai brought me food whenever he could, but often
he had nothing for either of us. One day I went to the

only local shop. They had three items for sale: a bag of dark gray salt, a cap with a visor, and the handle of a spade. When Minka, my friend from Moscow, realized how I was living, she started sending me all the money from her university grant. I went to pick it up at the beginning of every month, and every time the woman who handled the mail shook her head and said in amazement, 'So, friendships like this still exist?'

"Nikolai and I weren't the only prisoners in our village. Every day I ran into dozens of deportees, among them an older woman with thick glasses who I later found out was Anastasia Tsvetaeva, sister of the poet Marina Tsvetaeva. She looked worn, with short gray hair that poked out from beneath her kerchief.

"Nikolai and I used to go for walks along the part of the path that led to the edge of the woods, which was as far as they'd let us go. We loved the early twilights in winter when the setting sun showed through the firs and larches. But in no time, Nikolai's inner guard warned us: 'Get back! We could wind up with a sentence of twenty years inside the Arctic Circle for going too far,' so we walked from the village to the woods, from the woods to the village, back and forth, back and forth, as though it were a prison yard.

"We went there on New Year's Eve too.

"'Do you know the legend of the Siberian Odysseus?'

"I didn't know anything about Siberia except Pikhtovka.

"Nikolai told me the tale of the mythic hunter Khanti-kho: Khanti-kho, the hunter, saddled two reindeer and went hunting with his son. For three years, they rode and rode until finally they found bear tracks. Khanti-kho ordered his son to go home, and he followed the bear on his own. At night, he built a fire and lay down. When he woke up in the morning, he spotted the bear climbing over some rocks in the distance. "Wait till you see what happens!" exclaimed Khanti-kho, mounting his reindeer and starting after the bear. He rode until he reached a village with wooden houses and saw that the bear was entering the first cabin. Khanti-kho followed.

When he got inside, there were four people waiting. "Where are you going?" asked one, an old woman. "Are you following the bear? You won't catch her because I am the bear." The three other inhabitants surrounded Khanti-kho. They were giants. "Hunter Khanti-kho," they told him, "you won't come out of here alive if you don't pass these tests: First, you're going to have a feast with us; then, you'll fight off a herd of reindeer, and finally, you'll bring us a flock of wild geese, either dead or alive. If you complete each task, we'll give you this beautiful young woman, Nai, as your wife."

"I won't marry beautiful Nai because I already have a wife, and besides she's too young for me. But she'd make a fine wife for my son."

For three days and three nights they ate roasted reindeer meat, washed down with plenty of vodka, and the giants fell asleep under the table. Khanti-kho kept on eating, because during the seasons he'd been following the bear, he'd never had enough food. The giants were happy with him. When winter came, they fastened skis onto their boots and took off after the reindeer. When they got to the plains, a herd of reindeer descended on them. Khanti-kho swung his ax so skillfully that after much fighting not one reindeer was left alive.

This happened with two more herds. "So far you've gotten off easily," the giants told him, "but wait until the wild geese come." When it was time for the geese to migrate, Khanti-kho again took up his ax. He raised his arm and within seconds the flock lay at his feet. The same thing happened with a second and third flock. The giants congratulated Khanti-kho for passing the three tests and said their good-byes. They prepared three sleds, laden with the goods that made up beautiful Nai's dowry—she was a rich bride—and hitched them to Khanti-kho's reindeer. Then Nai, Khanti-kho, and his reindeer set off across the wilderness. After a long trip, they arrived home. Nai asked, "Where is the huge herd of reindeer? I see only two old things here." Just then a handsome young man came out of the woods, with a little boy and a huge herd of reindeer trotting behind them. "Who's that? A thief who has stolen my reindeer?" shouted Khanti-kho as he turned to them. The little boy was frightened. He was about to run when the young man stopped him. "Papa is back! It's Papa, who's been away for a long time. You weren't even born yet when he left. We had gone out hunting together but we separated and nobody expected him to come back. Mama will be so happy!" The little boy ran to the house, shouting, "Mama, Mama, Papa is back!" But his mother didn't believe him. "Papa? I don't think so. The wild animals are probably feeding on his bones somewhere." Even when Khanti-kho was at her side, she kept looking at him like a stranger. Then he embraced her and said, "I didn't bring the bear back, but I did bring a wife for our son. I wish you great happiness, my children."

"Yes, my life really has become a Siberian odyssey, I thought.

"While Nikolai was telling me this story, the moon ducked behind the clouds from time to time, but now it came out in all its brilliance. Under its silvery light, the snow on the fir trees looked like cotton, and the snowflakes sparkled a thousand colors. Nikolai and I realized that it was midnight when we heard the sound of voices from the village. We wished each other a happy new year, and we kissed.

"Afterwards it took me a long time to fall asleep. Imagine, I thought, celebrating the new year on the taiga! I was worried about my future, but at the same time I didn't want anything to change right now. I didn't want to be separated from Nikolai. I prayed that the authorities would ignore the request I'd put in to be relocated."

{9}

But the authorities accepted my request. Back in Butyrka Prison, when I had just learned that I would be deported to Siberia for five years while my sister Gaira had been condemned to Kazakhstan, I immediately requested a transfer so that I could be with her in the south, with an easier climate. At the beginning of May, I was notified that my request had been granted and that I should go directly to Kazakhstan. Otherwise, I'd be considered a runaway.

"I dealt with all the procedures slowly and calmly. After all, I had been given ten days to get there. But Nikolai gave me an urgent warning: 'No matter what happens, you have to be in Kazakhstan in ten days. Otherwise, they'll denounce you for trying to escape. If you don't get there in time, they could easily send you to some place beyond the Arctic Circle for twenty-five years. That would be a slow death.'

"I took the official form that said I was expected at the camp in Kazakhstan on May 17 and went to see a local man with a tractor about taking me the sixty kilometers to Petropavlovsk, where I could catch the train. He agreed. 'I'll take you. Come tomorrow at six.'

"The next day, at six in the morning, it turned out that the tractor was broken down and had to be fixed. 'Come back at twelve,' he told me.

"At twelve, the tractor was still not working. The same thing happened the next day. I only had eight days left. I decided to walk to the train station.

"'Sixty kilometers on foot!' Nikolai was horrified. 'And alone! I can't go with you because they'd condemn me as a runaway.'

"'I'm doing it.'

"'The taiga will be covered with mud now because of the melted snow, and it will be freezing at night. There will be piles of melting snow everywhere.'

"But my mind was made up, and I left on May 9. Nikolai accompanied me to the edge of the village. We said good-bye there. When I had walked a good way, I turned around like Lot's wife. I saw the village in the distance, and on the edge of it I thought I saw the figure of a man. Maybe it's just my imagination, because it's what I want to see, I told myself. But I also thought I heard the tender melody from the first movement of Mendelssohn's *Violin Concerto*."

{10}

I walked easily; I was carrying only a backpack with a chunk
of bread, soap, a towel, and a few small provisions. In my
hand, I had a cane that I could lean on or use as a weapon if
I had to. At five in the afternoon, I reached Orlovka, where
I thought to spend the night. I picked the house that was in
the best condition. In the doorway stood a little girl wearing a
summer dress, even though there were still a few damp snowflakes floating in the air.

"I asked her if they could sell me a glass of milk. The
woman who was in charge gave me the milk. I shared my piece
of bread with her, and when I was done, I left a ruble on the
table. The little girl grabbed it and ran off. 'You little thief,' the
woman said without much effort.

"'Do you think I can reach the next village before nightfall?'

"The woman just shrugged her shoulders. I left and kept
walking through the muddy flatland and over the piles of
snow of the taiga. The wet snowflakes floated in the air while
I marked my rhythm with my cane. I took in everything that
surrounded me, happy to be free for a week. After a while, I
saw something dark in the distance. 'Is it a man or a wolf,' I
wondered, hoping it was a wolf. When the figure got closer,
I saw that it was a man. Should I greet him like people do in
the country, or would that be risky? 'Good afternoon,' the
man greeted me first. I answered with the same words. He
drew away into the distance.

"The next morning when I started off again, I could no longer remember the name of the village where I had spent the

night. Around midday I approached a wood. That's what they had told me in Pikhtovka: 'You'll cross a wood; always stay on the same road; don't turn off any time or you'll get lost.' But the path forked. They hadn't warned me. I wondered for a minute which path would lead to the station and decided to take the one on the left. The path led me to some train tracks. I followed them in a westerly direction, eventually arriving at a station. It was nearly deserted, but I saw a girl and asked her if the train that was heading west would be coming soon.

"'It's just gone,' she was dressed almost exactly like I was except for a kerchief that she wore knotted like they do in the country.

"'Just now?'

"'No, about half an hour ago.'

"So, if I'd taken the right fork on the path, I would have gotten there on time!

"'And when is the next one coming?'

"'The day after tomorrow.'

"The day after tomorrow? So, the trains don't pass very often! Nikolai was right: this trip was crazy! When the train finally came, I would only have four days to get there, and I had to cross half of Siberia! And how would I spend the time until then?

"'Where are you going?' she asked me.

"'To Karaganda.'

"'To see your family? And where did you come from?'

"I was thinking about the train I'd just missed and not about my answer. Without giving it a thought, I said, 'From Moscow.'

"The girl started laughing. She liked the joke.

"'Well, in fact, I'm coming from Pikhtovka.'

"'Ah, I've heard of it, but I've never been there.' Then she took a key out of her pocket.

"'Look. Do you see that house over there? When you go in, tell them that you've come to see Frosa. There's a bed. Take a rest. And there's a purée on the table. It'll be cold by now, but at least you'll have something to eat.'"

{11}

The last car on the Vladivostok-Moscow express swayed from side to side, but I liked that. I had a seat, the windows weren't barred, and even if I looked a little different from the other passengers because of my Siberian work clothes (I had sold my party clothes—the blouse with the buttons, the straight black skirt, the high heels—some time ago), I was free, and I had the same rights as anybody else.

"A well-dressed young woman with a little boy started up a conversation with me, and she offered me some buns with our tea. On the table, for everybody to share, I placed a chocolate bar—a luxury I hadn't tasted in a long time—that Nikolai had given me for the trip. The young mother got off soon after, and then the ticket collector came and cleaned the table. She took almost the entire chocolate bar and then, as if unconsciously, stuck it in her pocket. I was about to tell her that the chocolate was mine, but I didn't. What good would it do? She would accuse me of calling her a thief and make a big scene.

"I had to change trains in Petropavlovsk. I joined a long line waiting to buy tickets, but I soon found out there were none left for Karaganda. I looked for a policeman.

"A man in uniform listened to my story and answered in a bored voice: 'What do I care? Do I look like the ticket clerk?'

"'No, but there are no tickets at the ticket window. I have to take this train. Otherwise, I won't get there on time, and they'll sentence me as a runaway.'

"'What do I care?' the cop answered, irritated.

"I got back in the line, which didn't move. In front of me was a grandmother with her grandson. She complained, 'It's the same old story. You need deep pockets to travel. And as for me here with my grandson, they must expect us to walk!'

"'You mean there's room on the train if you have money?' I asked her.

"'They've just announced it on the loudspeaker. There are only first-class tickets left for the Karaganda train,' the old lady explained, pointing to the next ticket window over, where only a few people were standing. At that window, half dead with fear, I managed to get out the words: 'A ticket for Karaganda.'

"I did have enough money! Not only that, they gave me change!

"I held on tight to the ticket and headed to the platform. 'It must be this train: Moscow-Balkhash.' The ticket collector looked at my muddy boots, my work jacket with the prisoner's number, my backpack, and my calloused hands. He examined my ticket so carefully he almost bit it.

"The train started up. I had hours to look at the countryside through a wide-open window, and in my ears, I still heard the sweet Allegro molto appassionato of the *Violin Concerto* that Nikolai had played for me so often."

{12}

"What happened after that?" I ask once Zayara has gone quiet.

"What happened after that?" she repeats as if she were waking up from a long sleep. "Nothing special. In Kazakhstan I finished my sentence of hard labor, and after Stalin's death, I returned to Moscow. I found a job, got married, had two children, led an ordinary life."

"It must have been wonderful to go back home after all that forced labor."

"Yes...but..."

"But, what?"

"My time in Siberia was so inspiring!"

"But you didn't have enough to eat; you couldn't even earn enough to live on; there was no comfortable place to sleep..."

"But I had real friends there, friends I could confide in. Since then, I haven't confided in anyone."

"And...you fell in love?" I ask after wondering if it's too personal a question.

Zayara isn't bothered. Just the opposite. She smiles with a sense of complicity. Then she holds her finger to her lips. I look and see that the door of the living room is open, and I realize that the Schubert quartet is no longer playing.

When we say good-bye, Zayara confesses to me, wistfully, "Even all these years later, I can still hear the Mendelssohn *Violin Concerto* in my head."

{13}

Zayara died two years after our meeting. I like to think that they played the Mendelssohn concerto at her funeral.

PENELOPE IN CHAINS

Susanna Pechuro

{1}

The front door of the apartment is open, just as Susanna
Pechuro had told me it would be when we spoke earlier
on the phone. The apartment itself is on the first floor in a
building on Leninsky Avenue. Susanna gets halfway up because, like many women who spent years in the Gulag, she
can't stand for very long. The women who suffered from malnutrition as young girls, when their bodies were forming, have
had serious mobility problems as they aged.

To shake the hand Susanna holds out to me, I make my
way through a heap of cats of every color. Susanna watches
me for a minute through big, expressive brown eyes. Then
she gets ready to feed her cats. I help her put food in a dish,
and the cats approach us, jumping over one another, to reach
the food. This task out of the way, Susanna sits down again,
calmly, and prepares to tell her story.

{2}

When I was fourteen, in an extracurricular course on literature, I met two boys who were a bit older than I. Boris and Vladik were inseparable friends. I used to call them Dobchinsky and Bobchinsky after the two comic characters in Nikolai Gogol's *The Inspector General.* Boris, who was tall and strong with a thick mat of curly hair, was a real scholar. He seemed older than sixteen. Vladik, who was delicate, unassuming, and ironic, had completely succumbed to his friend's charm. I, too, would soon come to recognize it.

"By that time, Boris had already lived a full life. His father had died in 1941 in the war, and his uncle had taken him to an occupied zone in Germany. The boy came back to Moscow when he was fifteen. He refused to live with his mother and stepfather. Instead, he opted for one of the rooms in a communal apartment on Manege Square. He used to invite me and other friends to his lair, and he'd lend us the books that were left from his father's library.

"Boris, our authority on political and philosophical questions, directed our studies. He wanted us to develop a real political culture, and he had us read the works of politicians and revolutionaries, whether they were Russian or foreign. The second edition of Lenin's complete works was a big hit. At that time, it had completely disappeared from bookstores and libraries, and you could only buy an edition that had been censored and corrected after his death. Sometimes in that room, Boris read us his own poems. Other times, Vladik read his stories. Vladik's real name was Vladlen, short for Vladimir Lenin. His parents had named his brother Leomar (*leninizin, oruzhe marxistov*: "Leninism, the arm of Marxism"). Both boys, obviously, came from orthodox and militant Marxist families.

"One day we got together at Boris's 'library.' Boris, who had inherited a piano, played one of Chopin's nocturnes. Afterward, we all had tea. It was almost summer, and I remembered how, on vacation in 1945, when I was eleven, I had gone to a Young Pioneers camp, in a school building dozens of kilometers away from Moscow. Trains passed by it. I told my friends that all the children made bouquets out of daisies, dandelions, and bluebells, and we'd give them to the soldiers who were going back home on the train. If the train stopped, we'd hand them the bouquets. If it kept on, we'd throw them in the windows.

"Boris sipped a little tea; then he said: 'I know a bit about the war, more than what's written up in the newspapers and what we learned at school. It's much more complicated than it seems.' He stopped talking.

"'Then, what *was* it like?' I asked, curious.

"'In 1945, when you were at camp, and in 1946, too, the trains didn't just carry the happy young people who were heading home after winning a war. In the cattle cars, they transported prisoners of war: Russians and Germans alike."

"I was confused. 'Where did they take them?'

"'To Siberia, to the forced labor camps.'

"With my eyes wide open, I shook my head. I had never heard anything about any camps other than the Young Pioneers camps where I'd spent my summers. Boris explained:

'The Soviet forced labor camps are extermination camps, just like the Nazi concentration camps. Besides the German and Russian prisoners of war, they transported thousands of other condemned souls, although there's no way of knowing just how many: people who lived in western Ukraine, in the Baltic states, and also Poles and Germans, apart from the Russians who had lived in those territories during the war.'

"'And why doesn't anyone talk about this?' I protested, indignant. 'Our teacher has never said a word on the subject.'

"'Because it's forbidden to speak publicly about it.'

"'But if you know about it, surely other people in Moscow know too!'

"Boris kept quiet.

"'It doesn't affect them,' said Vladik. 'Why put out a fire if you're not getting burned?'

"I thought that it *did* affect me and that I would ask my teacher and talk about it with my friends."

{3}

Susanna takes a break and pets a black cat. Then she turns to me and says slowly, as if it were hard for her to speak:

"One afternoon in January, my father came home from work, back to the little room that the four of us in my family shared in the communal apartment we had in Moscow, in Arbat. His face was gray. He almost had to force himself to come into the room, but he managed to say, 'They've killed Mikhoels.' Mikhoels, who in 1948 was fifty-eight years old, was the lead actor in the Jewish theater where the plays were performed in Yiddish, the language we spoke at home.

"He sat down heavily in his chair. When he had stopped crying, he said in a very low, careful voice: 'This murder will unleash a bacchanal, "the struggle against cosmopolitanism," as they've started calling it. You'll see.'

"'What's "the struggle against cosmopolitanism"?' I asked, dumbfounded, with what little voice was left to me.

"'It's a euphemism for the official policy of anti-Semitism that the government is encouraging. A campaign of xenophobia all of Russia will join in.'

"In the weeks that followed, I could see for myself how our history was being falsified. At school, they began to teach us that everything important in the world had been done by the Russians, that the great discoverers were all Russians, just like the great writers, painters, and composers. The students protested. They didn't want to overlook names like Newton, Shakespeare, and Beethoven. One morning, Nikolai Kravchenko, my old physics professor, said very insistently: 'Russia has contributed great riches to world culture. We don't need to appropriate foreigners' contributions, so remember this: the steam engine was invented by James Watt.'"

{4}

That afternoon I told Boris and Vladik about the brave physics teacher. They told me that the Soviet government had organized a campaign against the intelligentsia, for example, against the poet Anna Akhmatova and the short-story writer Mikhail Zoshchenko, and also against the composers whom they were calling 'formalists': Sergei Prokofiev and Dmitri Shostakovich.

"We kept talking until well into the night. As usual, we had made strong black tea. When we ran out of sugar, we drank it with honey. The boys taught me about the dogmas of pseudo-Communist doctrine that they'd filled our heads with at school, in the Young Pioneers organizations, and in the Komsomol, the Communist youth union; doctrines that were propagated all over with much ado: slogans in newspapers and magazines, on the radio, and on posters in the street.

"Afterward, they walked me home through the quiet, dark streets of Moscow. During this nocturnal walk, Boris, who was an authority for us whether at home or in school, decided to form his own organization one day.

"'When?' I was interested.

"'When the time is right. The whole point will be to save our old revolutionary values from the people and tendencies that betray our principles.' His voice resounded through the silence of the night.

"'Hurrah!' I shouted. I realized that this would mean seeing him even more often. I also realized that our plan was honest and, above all, that it was exciting, because it would mean doing something that was forbidden. At that time, I didn't even know the word 'dissident.'"

I notice that Susanna's eyes are shining. They seem to give off little sparks every time she mentions Boris.

"Boris's influence grew at school. In the extracurricular course on literature, he almost always had the last word, and the woman in charge, one of the teachers, began to worry. She announced that before reading a poem or story in class, the students had to get her approval. But nobody paid any attention to her, and the course continued as usual."

{5}

One afternoon in 1950, I was at school looking out the window, watching snowflakes shine in the light of the streetlamp. (By that time, I was sixteen.) One of my classmates read some verses she had written recently. It was a short, melancholy poem about a student gathering. All of us liked it, except the teacher, who jumped up and announced in a voice with a cold edge: 'This poem is anti-Soviet!'

"'But why?' I was surprised.

"'Why? Don't you see it's sad? Some feelings are not meant for Soviet youth.'

"'But we're all sad sometimes,' I objected.

"'Soviet youth should never be. Sadness is decadent,' the teacher cut me off.

"My two friends and I protested. It had no effect. That's how things went. We announced that we were dropping the course, since it wasn't obligatory anyway, and that instead we'd get together at Boris's house. There we could recite what we liked and talk about literature.

"Boris was eighteen by then, and he was someone people paid attention to. He planned to take his entrance exams the following year to study in the School of Philosophy at the Moscow City University. Vladik was nineteen and in his first year in the School of Medicine at the university.

"Boris wanted us to read Russian literature from the Silver Age. Alexander Blok, Anna Akhmatova, Andrei Bely, Osip Mandelstam, Marina Tsvetaeva, Nikolai Gumilyov, and other poets who had published at the end of the last century and into the 1920s and 1930s were forbidden now. Younger students, who were now attending Boris's literary gatherings in addition to the extracurricular class on literature, talked enthusiastically about these new discoveries. They meant well, but the woman in charge of the extracurricular course denounced her former student to the Ministry of Internal Affairs.

"Not long after that, Boris, who didn't trust anything, found listening devices in his house. They had installed them on the pretext of checking the electrical system. But that didn't scare us. It was too cold to go to the park, so we inserted a heavy sheet of paper in the electric fan and turned it up to full blast so that it was impossible to hear our conversations. We whispered as well. The incident just reinforced our friendship.

"At the end of the summer, the two boys came to see me. I had just turned seventeen and was spending a few weeks of my vacation in my grandmother's old wooden house, out in the country. There, on the veranda, they told me. What they told me was so important that I never went back to the sort of life I'd lived in the past and which I'd found so comfortable.

"My grandmother had fixed an apricot pie for us. Vladik couldn't stop eating. Boris had a bite and then wiped his lips. He didn't eat any more.

"'Susanna, we've decided it's time to form, seriously now, the secret organization to combat the Stalinist regime.'

"I waited to hear what would come next.

"'We've come just to share our plans with you. We'd like to make you one of the members, but we can't. It's too dangerous.'

"I was enthusiastic. It seemed very romantic to me. That summer I had read four volumes of the complete works of Stalin—a friend had sent them as a birthday present—and they didn't have the answer to any of the social problems that concerned me. But even more than that, I wanted to stay by Boris's side.

"Three months earlier, in May, while taking a walk together, Boris had told me that we had to separate. He was preparing to create an illegal organization that the administration would not look on kindly, and our friendship could put me in danger. With those words, he walked me home and kissed me perhaps for the last time. I spent two weeks without eating or sleeping, then I headed to Boris's house, and outside the door of his room I blurted out: 'There's no way we can separate!'

"Now, at the end of summer, on the veranda with apricot pie and the inevitable cup of tea, my stomach churned again. Quickly, without giving it any thought, I said, 'You can count on me, Dobchinsky and Bobchinsky!'

"The boys said nothing. Finally, after taking another piece of pie and licking his lips, Vladik said: 'It's dangerous,

Susanna. Do it only if you're totally convinced. And maybe not even then.'

"Boris, very serious and speaking in a low voice, added, 'It will cost us our lives, Susanna. You can be sure of that. It's not for you.'

"'It's not for me?'

"'Absolutely not.'

"'Then why did you tell me? Why did you come? What are you doing here?'

"I wasn't happy with the conversation. I knew Boris was a hero, but I wanted to do great things too, I didn't want to be left behind! And I wanted to be worthy of him. When the boys left, I told myself that whatever happened, I would follow Boris and Vladik. But if I did, I would have to leave my grandmother, her veranda where I loved to sunbathe, and my walks in the woods. I could no longer be part of the Komsomol, I who loved participating in all the activities of my youth organization because I believed in them, and I honestly tried to do everything I could for my country. I wanted to be a teacher like my old physics professor, who refused to disown Newton and Watt. And what would happen to my parents and my little brother? If I was imprisoned, they would stop laughing over dinner. And if they were imprisoned? I couldn't bear it. I would not be able to forgive myself if my family suffered because of me. The next day, I would tell the boys that I wasn't up for it. I made up my mind, and then I went to bed.

"But I woke up in the middle of the night. Could I keep on living without Boris? Without his eyes, his arms, his hands? Without his conversations? Without our tacit understanding?

"I argued with myself for a long time, even though I knew in my heart that my mind was made up.

"More people joined the secret dissident organization: handsome Zhenia; little Vladimir, who was fragile and like-able; Irina, whose parents had been imprisoned for no reason for a long time; Katya, who already knew what the Siberian forced labor camps were like since she and her mother had been condemned to them years ago; and Maya, whose parents were sentenced to decades in Siberia. As time went by, more and more people joined. With his usual clarity and concision, Boris wrote up statutes for the organization so it could struggle with the revolutionary question.

"We all celebrated New Year's Eve together. We said good-bye to 1950 and wished each other good luck in 1951."

{6}

At the beginning of January, I went with Boris to the train station. He was going to spend a couple of weeks at his uncle's house in Leningrad in order to tell his friends there about the dissident organization. He was arrested on the night of January 17.

"In the early morning of January 18, the secret police arrested Vladik. And that night they came for me."

Susanna stops as though she doesn't want to keep on talking. She gets halfway up, grabs a tricolor cat and holds it on her lap so she can pet it, but the cat immediately jumps up to get comfortable in a corner of the living room. Susanna follows the animal with her eyes, but then she comes back to reality and goes on with her story.

"For four hours, three secret policemen went over our papers, looking for forbidden texts, and they tore our room apart. For four hours, they took out all my textbooks and notebooks, and they took all the clothes out of the closet. My little brother, in my mother's arms, spent the four hours shouting, 'Make those men go away!' My father had a minor heart attack. The porter, half asleep in the doorway, watched the whole catastrophe.

"My mother packed up warm clothes and wool socks for me. Before leaving, I looked carefully at the room with the feeling that I would never see it again. At that moment, a period of my life was ending. As a memento, I grabbed my favorite doll.

"'You'd better leave it,' one of the secret police shouted at me. 'That doll would be the icing on the cake. Dolls! Prison isn't a nursery!'

"Sitting in the back seat of the car between two policemen, I wondered if everyone else had been arrested. 'What will become of Dobchinsky and Bobchinsky?' I worried over and over. And I swore to myself that in the interrogations I wouldn't give anyone away or mention any names."

{7}

I saw very clearly how the inmates in the collective cells at Lubyanka Prison opened their mouths and rubbed their eyes when I appeared in the doorway, a seventeen-year-old with braids, wearing a carefully ironed child's dress with a white collar. I riddled them with questions: Why had they been arrested? Where were they from? Was there any way to get out?

"The women patiently explained to me that in most cases the arrest didn't have a clear reason and that, except for communism, political parties were banned. During the next fourteen days, while they humiliated us in every way imaginable—lying to our faces, tricking us, terrifying us, and not letting us get a wink of sleep—my new companions gave me a whole course on survival in prison. I learned to communicate from one cell to another by knocking on the wall, to make needles from the spines of the fish that floated in the concoction they called soup. I learned to sleep not just while I was sitting up, but even with my eyes open so that the guard did not realize what was happening. Those are just a few of the things I learned during my first two weeks of prison.

"When it was almost time for my trial, the investigators showed me what they had written about me. My signature appeared under the wildest stories, from an attempt to assassinate Stalin to a plan to blow up the Moscow Metro.

"On February 7, 1951, in the basement of the Lefortovo Prison, they held a trial for me and the group of dissidents to which I belonged. The military department of the Superior Court of the USSR judged us. Detainees had no right to a defense. On the night of the thirteenth, the verdict was announced.

"Boris, Vladik, and handsome Zhenia were condemned to the longest sentence possible. Katya, Irina, and I were each sentenced to twenty-five years in forced labor camps. The verdict was a major shock. Any plans for the future were off the table. But I only thought about one thing: if Boris would survive."

{8}

I n 1952 they transferred us to forced labor camps. Irina and Ida, two girls from Boris's organization, were sent to what was called the Steplag Camp, in Kengir, Kazakhstan, where they would witness the 1954 uprising. Several thousand deportees rebelled after a group of prisoners was executed, supposedly for not respecting the rules. The uprising lasted forty days. During that time, the insurgents appealed to a committee in Moscow to investigate the case and establish more humane conditions. In June of 1954, more than a year after Stalin's death and after the arrest and execution of Beria, the chief of the secret police, the uprising was crushed. Without any warning, tanks drove across the camp, which was filled with unarmed people, more women than men. The survivors, including Irina and Ida, were moved to another, much harsher camp, well inside the Arctic Circle. To get there, they had to cross all of Siberia, heading north.

"As for me, back in 1951 the Ministry of Internal Affairs had begun arresting Jewish scientists, artists, and writers en masse and deporting them to labor camps. They determined that the dissident group I'd been in with Boris was a 'Jewish Nationalist' group organized by Zionists. For that reason, during my first years in the Gulag I suffered constant interrogations and was frequently moved from one area to another. In total, I was in eleven prisons and seven work camps or penitentiary camps.

"Every time they transferred me to a different Gulag, I hoped to hear something about Boris, to find out where he had been sent. I asked everyone I could about him. From time to time, there was a spark of hope: someone would say they had seen him doing forced labor in Kolyma, or in Vorkuta or Norilsk; but someone else would assure me they'd seen him in prison. I held on to those bits of news as if they were treasures.

"I was grateful for the old inmates, prisoners who had been made wise by their lives and misfortunes. Those brave women had witnessed events that we young ones only knew about from history or the falsified accounts that textbooks and newspapers reported. In the camps, the old women opened our young eyes to the true history of our country.

"In April 1952 they pushed me into a crowd of women jammed into a train with barred windows. The train, overflowing with women—and some men, in other cars—set off at first in a southerly direction, toward Ryazan, where it stopped for a few hours before turning due north toward Siberia. The farther we traveled, the more snow we saw. I looked at the countryside through the bars of the window, fascinated by its beauty and brilliance. After a week of traveling, with no toilets, the train spit out hundreds of filthy, reeking, exhausted prisoners in the city of Inta. From there we had to walk to a particularly harsh work camp. It was said that few people came out alive.

"When I had been there a few months, I met a foreign woman with dark hair who must have been about fifty and was clearly connected to artistic and intellectual circles.

"'Have you seen Boris?' I blurted out.

"The lady looked at me compassionately, convinced that the little girl with braids had been driven mad by her suffering. Boris was a common Russian name. I realized the impression I must have made so I added quickly: 'I mean Boris Slutsky. Young, smart, dark-haired. A philosopher.' Lina—who was Spanish—gave it a moment's thought and then shook her head.

"Later I found out that Lina was Sergei Prokofiev's wife, but though she must have been proud of her husband, she never boasted about it. Thanks to her, I became part of a literary circle. Even after our twelve-hour work shifts, we would get together to read; this was more satisfying than sleep. In our improvised book club we read our own poems aloud or the poetry and prose of our great writers, with an emphasis on the ones who were forbidden, like Tsvetaeva and Zoshchenko. Nobody knew if they were alive or if they had died in the Gulag. I usually recited something by Anna Akhmatova.

"I will never forget Lina, a strong, tenacious, unfortunate woman. When I met her, she was peeling potatoes. She spent four years doing that. She would get up at six in the morning, take hold of a blunt knife (there was no other kind in the kitchen), and stick at the work until nightfall, peeling a huge pile of hard, half-frozen potatoes that were, truly, impossible to peel, potatoes that were the staple food of the whole camp of women and the neighboring camp of men. And every other day she'd also go to the woods to throw out the garbage from both camps. Though she was tiny and fragile, she did the work of several strong men. What eventually undid that delicate, unimaginably sensitive woman wasn't the hard conditions, however, but losing her voice. Besides being Prokofiev's wife, she was a soprano in her own right and had sung as a soloist in operas and concerts, and now she couldn't even sing solo roles in the performances we put on in the camps. She could only sing as part of the choir. Even more than the constant struggle of life in the camp, that's what made her so sad.

"The cultivated, educated women got more out of life than the other girls, and Lina even more. She was a person apart. You could see that she had a rich inner life; she radiated beauty, energy, and mental vitality even when she was sad and, like most of the women, suffered from depression. She was living through a nightmare.

"But she still saw beauty around her, something that most of us could not manage. During the winter in the Arctic Circle, when the sun doesn't come out for six months, Lina would suddenly stop and look at the sky: if it was clear, the aurora borealis would unfurl like a big, lazy animal, and the stars paled beside it. When spring was close and a dark red sky illuminated us for a couple of hours each day, Lina drank it in like a wanderer in the desert who has finally found water. In the autumn, when she went to the woods to throw away the garbage, she never tired of admiring the little yellow larches, the only trees that grew there. In fact, they were more like dwarf pines. She used to say that she should have been a painter so she could share all the shades of yellow. In the summer, she picked wildflowers without paying attention to the mosquitoes and huge flies that bit us. Afterward, she'd divide those flowers up with us; she always shared whatever she had. When she got a package from her children (we were allowed one package a year, which the guards picked over first), she shared everything that was left equally with her friends.

"Lina was always different. I remember that, for a long time, she shared a cell with a dancer. Even though she was exhausted from working all day, instead of taking to her bed, she did exercises with the dancer. That's why, unlike most of us, she didn't lose her flexibility.

"In the camps, each person had only herself to rely on, her identity and her sense of morality. And that also meant taking care of her appearance. At night after twelve- and even fifteen-hour work days, many women took care of their hair and helped each other comb out the lice; they used their hands to 'iron' their pants, the only pair they had for work and for sleep; and they cleaned the mud off boots that would be covered with mud again the next day (the mud was part of summer; in the winter there was nothing but ice and snowbanks as tall as two people). The women who took care of their appearance were careful to be well behaved, and their good influence spread to the others, at least the ones who were more receptive.

"Later they sent Lina and me to different camps. They did it so that the prisoners would not form deep friendships."

{9}

From Inta they sent me back to Lefortovo Prison in Moscow. This involved almost a month shoved up against other women in a train car in the worst conditions. People did their business in a bucket only at the beginning; toward the end, most of the women just used a corner.

"From Lefortovo, they sent me to Butyrka. It was 1953 then, and I heard that Stalin had died. My first thought was: now they'll let Boris go. And me too. We'll probably see each other soon! This hope shone on the horizon, but as the weeks and the months went by without any change, it finally burned out. I was hoping to find out something about Boris in the interrogations. Sometimes I couldn't bear any more, and I asked about him myself, but I never got good news. I couldn't accept the idea that Boris was dead. My memories of him were like a star of possibilities in the dark, cloudy sky of the future. This star guided me through all my suffering and my years of humiliation.

"From Moscow they sent me once again to the Siberian camps."

{10}

In late 1955 they sent me back to the prison in Moscow to reexamine my case. I had no hope that I'd be freed or that anything good would come out of the new investigation, but I did resume thinking that I might learn something about Boris.

"On April 26, 1956, they told us that our twenty-five-year sentences would be reduced to five years. Like many others, I had already spent more time than that in prisons and camps. As for Boris, they told me that he had been executed on March 26, 1953, three weeks before the death of Stalin. I did not entirely believe them.

"When they freed us, the camp authorities asked us to sign a document agreeing not to talk about what we had seen and lived through during our years of imprisonment. I refused to sign. They threatened me, but I didn't give in. I knew they couldn't detain me: I had been freed.

"I went home. It didn't make sense, but I almost expected to see Boris. For months and months, I looked for him on the street and in the metro."

{11}

Getting used to everyday life was incredibly hard. It was hard because everyone embraced me with open arms. My parents and my friends celebrated my return, and I was surrounded with love and care. Spirits were high; there were lots of parties. Baskets of flowers filled the room where I was living again with my parents and my little brother; and they spilled over into the entrance of the old communal apartment. Every day I was sent congratulatory letters and poems. And, despite all that, I felt empty inside.

"It seemed trivial, meaningless. Nobody who had always lived in freedom could even remotely imagine what I had been through. It seemed to me that they hadn't really lived. They had no experience of life, not what I would call experience. Their world was completely different from mine. I felt alone, with no one to understand me.

"In the street I saw men and women without a worry in the world, teeming into cafes for a cup of tea or a glass of wine. I was struck by their trivial conversations about the weather or the latest style, laughing just because they were happy to be alive. I saw the display windows of stores, filled with baubles in every color, the children shouting while they played with a ball in the street, the telephone boxes where people arranged to meet their lovers, all of them happy and unconcerned. Cars and trolleys zipped past me. Streetcars honked. Men bought bouquets of violets and lilies of the valley for their girlfriends; others waited in line to buy meat to take home for dinner. Lots of people ate without waiting, buying juicy frankfurters with mustard from the stands that lined the streets. People rushed down the wide avenues and streets or sat on a bench in the park to lick a tasty ice-cream cone topped with whipped cream or fruit. My old friends were having a ball. The Khrushchev era gave them a little more freedom, and the young people in the cities went to film clubs to see pictures by Roberto Rossellini and Federico Fellini and to cafes where they could listen to jazz, but it was painful to see them. I could not forget, even for a minute, what they didn't want to see: that under that calm surface a vicious regime lay in wait, a brutal political machine that watched constantly and that, like an evil dragon, devoured its victims every day.

"Around then they talked about the 'thaw' Khrushchev's new politics had brought, but I knew, and often said, it was just a mask to cover the brutish face of the regime. My parents didn't understand why I was so sad. They believed that after a long separation their little girl had been returned to them, but the person who went home was a grown woman who had little in common with the child, a woman who in less than six years had lived more than other people live in their whole lives, who had come to know the cruel face of life and had spent years on the frontier between life and death.

"In the first year, especially, after my return, I spent as much time as I could in the company of women who had also been detainees, who had had the same experiences I did, and who, like me, recoiled at normal life. My old friends organized get-togethers for me, where young poets read their work, but I felt like a foreigner in their midst, and I finally stopped going.

"After a long time, I came to value at least part of my experience. I realized that it was in the camps where I had learned to recognize the profound evil my country had engendered. The work camp was my most important lesson. Those bitter, hard years were my best school, a school that would help me throughout the rest of my life. I can't imagine my life without the camps. More than that: if I had to live my life over, I would not want to avoid that experience. Why? Because the most horrible struggles led to the strongest of friendships. There's no place for that kind of bond in normal life. It takes the most extreme situations to create that kind of love and solidarity."

{12}

I returned to my studies as if I were starving. Less than a month after I was freed, I presented myself for the entrance exams. Once I had passed them, I enrolled in the School of History at the University of Moscow in order to continue the scientific work Boris had wanted to dedicate himself to. I knew my friend had decided to specialize in Ivan the Terrible, the czar who transformed Russia from a medieval state into an empire, albeit at tremendous human cost, especially during the so-called *oprichnina* [the czar's policy of mass repression of the aristocrats].

"I passed the entrance exams, but they would not accept me. The dean, who knew where I had been, called and told me, 'We do not educate prison fodder in this school.'

"My new friends did what they could so that he would revoke the resolution. They knew how important it was for me to study, to start a new life. They were finally successful: the official from the Central Committee of the Communist Party of the USSR who was responsible for making the decision was a former detainee who had done his sentence in Abez, one of the camps where I had spent time. They finally accepted me in the School of History and Documentation.

"I threw myself into my studies, just as if I were devouring a piece of bread. In life I have experienced not only physical but also intellectual hunger. In one of the camps, they let us borrow books every ten days. I learned entire stories, articles, and essays by heart. For years after that, I fed on them."

{13}

On my first day at the university, the students were divided according to the historical period that we wanted to study. The fine historian Sigurd Schmidt asked me: 'You're going to study Ivan the Terrible? Then come to my office after class.' Once I was there, he said only one thing to me: 'Avoid historical analogies, because they keep you from really knowing the material.'

"I asked about Boris Slutsky again at the Ministry of Internal Affairs. They told me the same thing again, and this time they showed me a document testifying that he had been shot. This time it said in 1952.

"After that I married a classmate from the School of Mathematics. We had two children.

"From the 1960s on I collaborated with the dissidents. In the 1960s and 1970s, after work, I copied Boris's essays for a *samizdat*—our underground literature. In that way, I participated in the protests against the regime, but I also felt that I was working with Boris. After all, he was one of the first dissidents.

"And I finally got to witness something I thought I would never see: the collapse of communism. The years between 1989 and 1991 were my happiest. We lived to see the downfall of our totalitarian regime, and we tried to support the new system as best we could. I enthusiastically attended all the meetings and demonstrations, and I felt happy among the hundreds of thousands of people who thought as I did and who went out into the streets of Moscow because they could finally express their beliefs.

"In the 1990s, after the disintegration of the USSR, the Memorial was founded, an institution for the preservation of the memory of the victims of communism. I became one of the first associates. I worked on its organization. I answered hundreds of letters that reached us from all over Russia, written by people who could finally write about their own lives and the lives of their friends and relations, all victims of totalitarianism."

At that moment, a young man came into the apartment without knocking on the door, just as other people had done throughout Susanna's narration. But the others had left when they realized she was being interviewed.

"This is my grandson Alexey Makarov, a student," Susanna looked at the boy with pride. "He studies, and at the same time, he works on the Memorial."

The boy shook hands with me and then sat down in a corner and began reading the opposition newspaper *Novaya Gazeta*. Susanna went on talking:

"And me? I've always done everything the way I think Boris would have wanted. He is still my light, just as he was before. I educated my children in that spirit, and now I am guiding my grandson. We all follow the teachings of Boris. In his interrogations, which I managed to read many years later at the KGB, Boris declared that everything he had done was for the good of the country, that he never thought about himself, but about the good of the people. That's what our parents and our teachers had taught us. Boris, like me, was the product of that education."

{14}

Lina Prokofiev was loyal to her husband too, even after he died. The two of us were rehabilitated, but Prokofiev, like my Boris, had died too soon. The Soviet secret services had torn the Prokofiev family apart. Soviet power liquidated Prokofiev and Boris in different ways but with the same result. After her rehabilitation, Lina dedicated the rest of her life to the preservation of her husband's work, first in Moscow, then in the West.

"Once I ran into her at a concert in Moscow. When she saw me, she ran up to embrace me, and she gave me her number so I could call her. She was so different, so bright and elegant and surrounded by artists, that I felt there was an abyss between her world and mine, and I was afraid that my call might be a bother. I didn't phone her, but I did think about her. I understood that Lina Prokofiev and her life were a metaphor for the twentieth century: it was the era of great advances in arts and sciences, and at the same time, the era of totalitarianism.

"I know that without my experience in the Gulag, I wouldn't be what I am today: a woman who is afraid of nothing. A person can turn into a monster in the camps, but if you come out of a camp and you don't become an ogre, you know that nothing in life can hurt you. You are armored. You've passed the test.

"My door is always open in case one of the children who play on the patio wants to come see me. And they come every day. I have cookies and candies ready for them. I don't lock my door at night, because sometimes one or another of my neighbors comes to chat. I couldn't get up to open the door for them. I can't walk as you can see."

Susanna leans over and pours a little milk from a bottle into a bowl for the cats. About ten of them come running, and, with their rough tongues, they lap up the drink. She turns all her attention to them, forgetting the world around her.

Susanna died the same way she lived: totally at the service of others, her neighbors and her cats... and the social justice Boris had died for.

A
TWENTIETH-CENTURY
JUDITH

Ella Markman

{1}

No! Really? You like Marina Tsvetaeva's poetry?"
Ella Markman's innocent, girlish voice sounds disparaging. While she talks, she is looking at the framed portrait that hangs on the living room wall. It shows a young Marina: a photograph of the poet when she was living in exile in Prague in the 1920s. Her head is resting gently on the head of her daughter Ariadna. They both have straight-cut bangs that cover their foreheads and form a line across the photograph. That was when Marina wrote "The Poem of the Mountain" and "The Poem of the End" about her love for and separation from a handsome young blond, a Russian like her. Marina didn't know at the time that she would soon move to Paris, and that there she would continue her correspondence with Rainer Maria Rilke, who was living in Switzerland near the Italian frontier, and Boris Pasternak, who was back in Moscow, and, using just her written words, she

would bewitch both. Nor did she know that at the end of the 1930s she would return to the USSR, following her husband Sergei Efron; that he would disappear in prison while Ariadna would be sent to the Gulag; nor that she herself would wind up in the grip of the NKVD, the secret police, who would push her to suicide.

"Ariadna Efron Tsvetaeva," I murmur.

"I knew her. In the forced labor camps," Ella says.

I would like to ask about Ariadna, but Ella stops to show me a bookcase filled with Marina's books. I open one of them: the margins are filled with penciled-in notes. I glance through the book. On the introductory page is a photograph of Marina that was taken during the years of her exile in Paris, when every morning she made herself a strong black coffee, took up her notebook, and wrote for hours when everybody else was still asleep. She didn't realize then that two years after returning to Russia she would be trapped. Ella's voice interrupts my reflections.

"My husband and I don't read Tsvetaeva. We don't understand why she had such an effect on men."

I answer that I don't know anything about that; the important thing is her poetry, but Ella doesn't give up on her argument.

"It's all there, in her verses!"

I don't want to argue, especially since I believe Ella is making fun of me: if she didn't like Marina's poetry, she wouldn't have so many of her books, with notes. I change the subject to Ariadna.

"What was she like?"

"A great beauty," Ella answers with the characteristic Russian admiration for feminine charm. "She had enormous eyes...like a lake at daybreak. Green, clear, and good. As she lost weight because of the forced labor, her eyes looked bigger and bigger. I have her correspondence with Boris Pasternak, the poet, who was a friend of her mother's."

On the bed where she invites me to sit, she places a typed notebook: a homemade, clandestine publication, a samizdat. While Ella slowly leaves the room to prepare tea, I open the notebook and begin to read.

{2}

August 26, 1949

Dear Boris,

The trip to the place where they sent me took four months and was exhausting. The leg from Kuibyshev to Krasnoyarsk was the hardest. The heat and our thirst were torture, and my heart ached as well. From Krasnoyarsk we went by boat up the Yenisey for what seemed like an endless voyage. Never in my life had I seen a river so big, so powerful, and, at the same time, so lazy. Its path was clear, and it headed to the north. I would never have planned to go see it on my own. The snow forest of the taiga on its banks began to change into a less wooded tundra. The cold came down from the north as though it were exhaled from the maw of some kind of extraterrestrial animal from time immemorial and, of course, to the end of time. Close to here, very close, there must be a kitchen where huge quantities of bad weather are cooked up and then sent out near and far. "A sudden cold front has set in," they tell us. The sunsets are beyond description. Instead of the feeling of fire, light, and heat that sunsets usually evoke, only a great creator could use so much gold and purple and, at the same time, transmit such an intense sensation of cold. It's below zero, and this is just August. What can we expect from now on?

They left me in the town of Turukhansk, three or four hundred kilometers from the Kara Sea. All the cabins are made of wood; there's only one stone building, an old monastery, which is ugly. Anyway, Turukhansk is a regional center, with schools, a hospital, and a club where films are followed inevitably by dances. In the streets, you find cows and stray dogs that pull sleds in the winter. I mean, the dogs pull the sleds; the cows just wander around.... This is a historic town. Y.M. Sverdlov, a Bolshevik party administrator and chairman of the All-Russian Central Executive Committee, was confined here. Our great Stalin, who was himself exiled in the next village, came to see him. Stalin was exiled to this area from 1915 to 1917. The old people around here remember both him and Sverdlov clearly. The little house where Sverdlov lived has become a museum, but I still haven't managed to get in. The hours I'm off must coincide with the hours the museum guard is off.

They gave me three days to find work, which is hard—and I mean very hard—to find here. For three days I knocked on every door looking for work and for coal. Just as I was getting desperate, I got lucky. They contracted me to do odd jobs in a school for a monthly salary of one hundred and eighty rubles. My duties are simple but varied. For twenty-two days, I harvested hemp on an uninhabited island; we used a kind of platform to transport ten tons of the stuff. The flies and mosquitoes stung my face so much they left me unrecognizable. Every half hour it rained, leaving the hemp and us wet. Then we dried out. We stayed in a tent that also got wet and dried out over and over. We didn't have much to eat, because we hadn't brought enough bread or oatmeal, not realizing what the weather would be like. Now I'm working on the renovation of the school: I do plaster work, paint the desks and the other furniture, scrub the endless floors, cut and saw firewood; in short, I work between twelve and fourteen hours a day.

The water we drink is from the Yenisey, which is not close, and we carry it, on foot, uphill. Because of all this, the way I look and the way I walk have become decidedly equine. I'm like one of the nags they used to use for transporting water, just like they're pictured in that famous manual of anatomy: hardworking, exhausted, and bony. But my eyes always take in the unrivaled beauty of Siberia. The images bypass my brain and go straight to my heart. My constant wild desire to write about and draw what I see here is equal only to my longing to go home. I don't have the time or the paper to capture these images, so I keep them in my heart, which is about to burst.

The conditions of life leave a lot to be desired. I rent a corner, worse than Dostoyevsky's, from an old woman who's not quite right in the head. There are cracks everywhere, and it's full of bedbugs. For this lovely little den with almost no heating, the old woman demands my whole salary. And for that amount, I don't *even have a place to sleep, since there's nothing but a stool and a table.*

I've just realized that for my whole life (I'll be thirty-six soon), I've never had my own room, a room where I could shut myself in and work without bothering anybody and without anybody bothering me. Worse yet, for the last few years, I've grown completely unaccustomed to seeing any place where a person could live in reasonable comfort. When I visited Vera Inber—the poet—at her home, I was depressed by the sight of the armchairs, armoires, sofas, and paintings, because they seemed so foreign to my experience. (On the other hand, I loved your house and wanted to touch it all with my hands.) In short, in these last years, I've become rough, and my life is reduced to basics. When the time comes—if it ever does—it will be hard for me to get used to the idea that I can do what I want and actually possess things of my own. Without being a total optimist, I'm still not convinced I'll be miserable for the rest of my life. I continue to dream that I'll wake up and life will be back to normal.

When I returned from the hemp harvest, I finally—after a long process—got my identity card. That's how I managed to get hold of the money you sent me. I thank you with all my heart. Please forgive me for cadging off you. Having to ask for help, even if it's from you, is horrible. Just like being in this damned cabin and crying, because I don't make enough to pay for feed and for a stall even though I work like a mule. Who needs my work? Who wants me to do this work? Boris, I always remember my mother. I remember her so clearly, and I dream about her almost every night. Maybe she can protect me if she's still alive.

When I got the money you sent me, I bought a warm jacket, a skirt, and some slippers. I'll also definitely get some felt boots. Besides that, I'll pay for firewood for the whole winter. I've already bought a little bit of every kind of food I could find here and ate it right away, like a character out of Jack London. I hope I'm not boring you with this chatter.

Dear Boris, your books stayed behind again, this time in the house in Ryazan. I beg you to put a few together for me. I always need to have your books close to hand. I would never willingly abandon them even though I've been forced to leave them behind. Please, please—if it's possible—send me every-thing you can put your hands on: your poems, your translations of Shakespeare, your prose. And "The Early Morning Trains," and, if you can, paper to write on and notebooks. We can't get them here . . .

Your very existence is a kind of miracle, my dear Boris! I am longing to receive news of you. Tell me about your life. Here the clouds often seem to have the same shape as your handwriting, so that the sky is like a page from one of your manuscripts. When that happens, I drop my yoke and buckets to read the heavens, and suddenly everything seems much happier. . . .

{3}

Sitting on the bed, waiting for Ella to come back for her interview, I mentally review what I know about Ariadna's life. In 1922, her father, Sergei Efron, had to leave the So-viet Union, and her mother, the thirty-year-old poet Marina

Tsvetaeva, along with ten-year-old Ariadna, escaped the hunger and repression there by moving to Berlin, where the family was reunited. They settled in Prague, which after the Revolution had become one of the biggest centers of Russian emigration, thanks to President Masaryk's help. In Prague, Ariadna went to a Russian school. In Paris, where the family moved after some years, she finished her studies at the prestigious School of Visual Arts in the Louvre and was involved with the *France-USSR* journal. As a painter, she had her first exhibition in Paris. It was praised by prominent artists like Natalia Goncharova.

Ariadna left home, in large part because she and her mother had violent disagreements that left them both feeling miserable. She went back to Moscow in March 1937—hoping to experience what she thought was a social and political miracle—just at the moment when the worst Stalinist purges were beginning. Ariadna, who was then twenty-four, was fascinated by the changes that were taking place in her homeland, changes that many of the Parisian intellectuals welcomed with open arms. In this sense, she was like her father, a man who had always felt the need to give himself up blindly to an ideal or a goal: after the Revolution, to the White Russians; then, later, to the Reds. It's interesting that, even after the incredible suffering Ariadna endured for seventeen years—she was tortured in prison and the Gulag and forced to perform the most menial and exhausting jobs in the far north—she never lost her belief in the Soviet Union.

A month and a half after Ariadna returned to Moscow, her father followed her. Like his daughter he had missed his homeland so much that in 1931 he asked the Soviet embassy in Paris for permission to return. When he was finally allowed back, the NKVD took advantage right away and recruited him for their secret service. And Tsvetaeva? Marina had no desire to return. But finally, under pressure from her family, she left Paris in 1939 and went back to Moscow with her son Mur to see Ariadna again and to take care of her husband, who was sick. When she was on the boat, she wrote, "After I boarded the ship, I stopped for a moment. I felt like Napoleon on the way to St. Helena." Marina realized, then, that there would be no return to Paris, that she would be exiled for good, and that this voyage would be the end of her freedom and perhaps of her very life.

Once she was in Moscow, Marina found out, right in the station, that her sister Anastasia and Anastasia's son had already been arrested. No one visited Marina or invited her to go out. In any event, very few people knew she was in Moscow. Not even her old friend, Boris Pasternak, one of the people closest to her, went near her house. Through an acquaintance, Pasternak sent greetings to Efron's sister so that she'd pass them on to Marina. That was it. By chance, the poet was at her sister-in-law's house at the time. The messenger passed on the greetings; her face tightened, but she didn't give the incident much weight. She knew that people were afraid of her. The sense of fear was everywhere. Later Pasternak, who spoke up for the victims of Soviet persecution, whom he called martyrs, was the only person to help her after Sergei and Ariadna were arrested, leaving her with a fourteen-year-old son and no money, no work, and no place to live. Thanks to his intercession, Marina moved to a house for writers and was given translating work.

Unfortunately, Marina never found out—because she didn't live to see it—that Pasternak exchanged letters with Ariadna and tried to help her when she was liberated from the camps and for a long time after when they sent her to the north of Siberia for what was supposed to be a life sentence laboring outside of the camps.

Did Marina imagine, in 1939, that her life would be different on her return to Moscow? She certainly knew it wasn't going to be a bed of roses, but she could not possibly have imagined the hell that awaited her. And Ariadna? Upon her return to Moscow, she worked in the Journalists' Union as a graphic artist and reporter. She met a young man, Samuil, who fell in love with her and moved into her house even though he was still married to his wife. It's hard to know if Ariadna realized that he worked for the NKVD, probably not. His superiors certainly sent him to spy on her—that's the only explanation for why officials allowed him to correspond with her and even visit her once in the Gulag, although they weren't married. Later Samuil fell out of favor, was arrested, condemned to death, and, in 1952, shot. Until that point, he had helped Ariadna and her relations as best he could.

Marina returned to a Moscow that was dominated by a panic caused by the repression, by the arrests and the deaths. Hysteria was part of the air they breathed. People went to bed with a suitcase prepared for prison or for Siberia. They were arrested and executed without hesitation or reason. In the summer of 1939, the whole family lived with people sent by the NKVD in a wooden cabin near Moscow. Their every movement was under strict control. Yet in spite of that, Sergei Efron, who had returned for his health, gradually recuperated thanks to the presence of Marina and the children. Then it happened.

A month and a half after Marina's return, on the night of August 27, somebody knocked at the door. Several members of the secret police conducted a thorough search of the house that lasted until dawn. In the morning they arrested Ariadna, but "even in those circumstances, she held her head up: she laughed and joked, if perhaps a little awkwardly," Marina noted. She didn't say good-bye to her mother or father or brother; she believed that she'd be back as soon as they cleared up the misunderstanding.

"Aren't you going to say good-bye?" Marina asked her.

Ariadna, who had finally started to cry, waved good-bye.

They locked her father up on October 10. A desperate Marina wrote to Lavrentiy Beria, the Minister of Internal Affairs. "My husband is very sick. I've lived with him for thirty years, and I've never known a better person." Along with other letters, this one went unanswered.

From that time on, Marina visited two prisons in Moscow. Her husband and her daughter were separated. She trembled with fear. After one of these visits, she noted, "My teeth were chattering so that I could not even say thank you when someone opened the door for me."

What was happening to the detainees in the meantime? In 1954, a year after Stalin's death, when conditions were a little easier, Ariadna presented an appeal to the public prosecutor for the USSR in which she described her experience of imprisonment: "When they shut me in, the people who interrogated me wanted me 1) to confess that I was an agent of the French intelligence service, 2) to confess that my father was aware of that, and 3) to confess that my father also belonged to the French intelligence service. They beat me from the beginning. They interrogated me day and night, even in the cell; they did not let me sleep; they shut me up in icy cells with no shoes and no clothes on; they beat me with rubber clubs known as 'interrogators for women'; they threatened to shoot me; and one time they even pretended to execute me."

Ariadna endured months of torture and psychological pressure to make her accuse her father of something he had not done. Once again, they took her back to her cell, with her face covered in bruises, only half conscious. A long time later, she wrote, "I couldn't believe I was the one who was withstanding all of this; I couldn't bear such treatment!" It sounds like a paraphrase of the verses written by Anna Akhmatova, whose son was also in a Stalinist prison and whose first husband was shot after the Revolution and the second sent to a gulag: "I am not that woman. It must be someone else who is suffering. I could never withstand it."

Finally, physically and psychically destroyed, Ariadna signed the paper they handed her.

After a year of suffering, interrogations, and torture in prison, they condemned her arbitrarily, without a trial, to seven years of forced labor in one of the strictest gulags.

Sergei Efron, never gave in, although they tortured him as much as they had tortured his daughter, perhaps even more.

He showed more willpower and character than he had ever before in his life. This is not uncommon among prisoners who know that they have nothing to lose, because everything is already hopelessly lost. They know that the last bit of humanity left to them, the only way they can still show they are human, is to assert their fortitude by not betraying their families or themselves. Efron's resolve was even more admirable, because he was in such a sorry state. After a desperate attempt to commit suicide, the prison psychiatrist wrote that "the prisoner suffers from hallucinations that are often auditory; he believes that somebody is talking about him in the hallway, that they want to arrest him, that his wife is dead. He suffers from anxiety and shows signs of depression and exhaustion; he thinks only about suicide, and he has an immovable conviction that something terrible will happen to him."

They shot him after two years in prison, a month and a half after his wife's death. Later they found a paper with his signature—deformed and illegible—that showed the condition he had been in.

In the meantime, Marina was left without the means to even feed her son Mur. No one wanted to provide work for a person who had emigrated and who was being persecuted by the NKVD. Everyone was afraid to associate with a woman whose husband and daughter were political prisoners. They were afraid of being accused themselves. The NKVD asked for her collaboration. If she didn't accept, they would make sure she never got a salary again. Marina refused. One of the last declarations she left was an application for work: "I beg you to give me a position as a dishwasher." The NKVD

ordered that it not be granted. The writer whom many con-
sider the finest poet of the twentieth century was then driven
to suicide.

In 1944 Mur, Ariadna's brother, died on the front, defending the country that had destroyed his family.

Ariadna didn't speak often about the work camps, but she
remembered the trip to the Gulag: they put her in a cattle car
that was filled with over fifty thieves and murderers. She was
twenty-eight at the time, and she realized right away what
would happen to her. Horrified, she fell to her knees next to
the locked door.

"What's your name?" the head of the thieves asked her.

In that atmosphere, her name sounded strange, like myth-
ological words from another world.

"So, you're Alochka!" the leader exclaimed joyfully.

It turned out that his lover had talked about Ariadna; they
had been cellmates in Lubyanka. Ariadna had helped her hide
various objects and had shared the food her mother sent to
the prison.

They made space for her on a cot and covered her with a
blanket. When they opened the cattle car a few days later, and
Ariadna came out alive, the guards couldn't believe their eyes.
They had sent fourteen women to the forced labor camps, and
only two had survived the trip.

Ariadna worked with the woodcutters inside the Arctic
Circle, in the Kizhi-Pogost camp, in the Komi Republic. In
the absolute darkness that lasted six months a year, with the
temperature at fifty below, she cut trees, split them with a saw,
and then piled them up.

That's where she learned about her father's death and also received one of the last letters from her mother:

You say what's hardest on you is happiness. The same thing is true of me. When something good happens, my eyes fill with tears, especially in public places. A single kind word will do it. Extreme vulnerability. I cry about everything. And then I open my mouth like a fish and swallow my tears. I overcome my emotions, but I start choking; people don't know where to look. . . .

Then the letters stopped coming. Ariadna asked all her relatives about her mother, but nobody told her anything. They were afraid to tell her the truth. She didn't find out for a long time—until an aunt finally admitted it two years after the fact—about Marina's death and, in 1944, her brother Mur's.

In 1947, once her sentence was completed, Ariadna, who had turned thirty-five and was skin and bones, with gray hair and a heart murmur, moved to Ryazan. The former detainees were forbidden to live within a hundred kilometers of Moscow, so they usually settled in the cities that were one hundred and one kilometers away. There, after a long bureaucratic process, she started teaching in an art school. Boris Pasternak sent her his translations of Shakespeare, and Ariadna read them to her dedicated students.

In 1949, however, they arrested her again and deported her to Krasnoyarsk, about a hundred kilometers from the Arctic Circle, sadly known for being the gulag closest to the North Pole. From there, Ariadna sent Boris Pasternak the letters that Ella had let me read while she prepared tea and a little something to eat. Ariadna had met Pasternak in Paris in 1935 when she was twenty-three. When he returned to Moscow, they saw each other more often. I am including a few of those letters here.

{4}

March 6, 1950

A few days ago the candidate for deputy of the Supreme Soviet made an official trip to Turukhansk. It was hideously cold, but the whole town ran out to meet him. The teenaged boys climbed up the posts and fences, the musicians rubbed their trumpets with alcohol to rehearse "The Soviet Hero" march. Workers and civil servants held up flags, portraits, posters, and signs, whose bright colors contrasted with the monotony of the snowy scene. At last, from the direction of the aerodrome, we could hear the tinkling of sleigh bells. We knew where the sound came from, but—because of the purity of the air and the echo—it seemed to be coming from all over at the same time. When the sleighs finally appeared, drawn by ponies with dense winter coats and high spirits, everyone shouted "Hurrah!" and threw themselves at the candidate. But it was hard to recognize him in the midst of all that confusion, especially since the men who formed his cortège, and there were a lot of them, all looked alike with their faces burned red by the cold. And they all wore sheepskin coats. For a minute I thought that at my age I wasn't up for that kind of celebration, but I couldn't help myself, and I started running too, without really knowing where, in the middle of the boys and their signs. I jumped over fences, sank into snow up to

*my knees, shouted "Hurrah!" and then went back to work, happy
as a lark, hoarse, my boots full of snow...*

*You know? I love every kind of demonstration, all the
popular festivals and even fairs. I adore the Russian multitude.
I've never enjoyed a play or any other form of "premeditated"
performance as much as a popular festival that overflows into
the streets of a city or a village—all the things my mother hated.*

April 17, 1950

*We've had three spring days in a row. The snow turns black, be-
comes porous and brittle; water drips from the roofs; warmish, gray
clouds slide across the sky. It will be a long time before the taiga
starts to turn green again, but it has taken on a bluish tint; it's
covered with a cream-colored haze, and when the sun sets behind
the woody fringe that marks the horizon, a faint penumbra de-
scends on the snow like the shadow of enormous eyelashes. Because
of the sunlight everything becomes malleable: the thin branches of
the larches, the branches of the fir trees, exuberant as a fox's tail,
so the outlines lose the dryness and sharp relief that are typical of
winter here. Everyone comes out into God's light: the children, the
puppies that were born in winter and raised in the huts, along with
the calves and the chickens. You still don't see or hear the birds,
except for one time when I caught sight of an odd flock of sparrows
with white pompadours and white bibs on their breasts.*

*It still surprises me that in the last years I don't live at all in
the winter: I survive it; that's all....I went to see the doctor today.
She told me that the condition of my heart doesn't correspond to
my age, and she advised me to rest more and to avoid worry and*

stress. With this idea in mind, she prescribed a ton of useless remedies. As I understand it, these things also have secondary effects. As far as rest and a stress-free life, you can imagine, and, as far as my heart goes, I believe it still has a lot of powder to burn.

I've always hated going to official places: police stations, clinics, offices, etc. I hate breathing in their particular smell, which is also official. Today I spent four whole hours in the clinic, waiting in line with the other patients: men with days-old beards, pale women with stringy hair, teenagers with freckles on their high cheekbones. Benches with the backrests polished by innumerable shoulders. Posters that proclaim, "We have survived cancer," and "Protect your children from summer diarrhea," polished by so many readings. Oh, I can't bear them, just like the whispered conversations about pains in the lower part of the chest, under the scapula, in the stomach, in the breasts, in the temples. Everything hurts! My heart hurts me, a dull, throbbing pain, but—after listening to other people's complaints—I begin to feel almost indecently healthy, and I want to shake off my stupor and take off running.

On the other hand, I love hotels, docks, and train stations! The sadness you find there is totally different. It's a lively sadness, with big, fine wings just about to become jubilant, don't you think? Its intensity is a form of happiness. The sadness of the waiting rooms is different; it's a sadness that they plucked the feathers off when it was still alive, a sadness without expectations (what a beautiful word!). It's not even sadness, but something like a fly, left over from the summer.

I'm just chattering on about nothing really. The noise, the crowding, and the discomfort don't bother me much, but I would love to talk with you, even for a few minutes. In fact, I'm dying to talk to you! Everything I'm going through would be easy if I didn't miss Moscow so much. Now, more than ever, this loss makes me terribly sad. I know I didn't live there long, only 'til I was eight and then three more years when I was grown. This anguish is almost like an unrequited love. I've traveled to, sometimes lived in, magnificent cities, which I've admired, but never really loved. Once I left them behind, they didn't leave any more trace in my memory than the set of a play.

But Moscow is truly the city of my soul, just as it was for my mother. It's my city, my only property, and I can't accept its loss. I dream—and this is true, not just something I've made up—about streets, alleyways, and passageways that could exist only in Moscow and nowhere else. But with all this in mind, I couldn't live in Moscow, because I would never want to take it for granted. If it were up to me, I'd live and work happily far from Moscow, in the north, even farther north than I am now. I would really live, really work, not as I have to at this point. I'd write books about those things that few people have the chance to see. I'd make a good job of it, I assure you. The far north is virgin territory for a writer; no one has really done anything worthy of the theme. Then I'd go to Moscow from time to time for a visit, to submerge myself in its atmosphere, before heading back north. As you can see, I can't stop saying "I would, I would"...

May 29, 1953

Although May is almost over, today is our first spring day, cold and blue. It's cold because of the chunks of ice coming down the river. From the other side of the window, you can hear what sounds like the roar of an ocean, powerful and lazy. From the time I was a child, the laziness of great expanses of water frightened me. A flame has more temperament than the Yenisey, which empties into the ocean, or than the ocean, which swallows up the Yenisey. The water is powerful and lazy, like death, and that's why I hate it and am afraid of it. Yesterday I saw a teenaged boy drown. He was on the bank, fishing for the tree trunks that were floating down the river. He had a rope with an iron hook on one end and was holding the other in his hand. When a trunk came down the river, he'd throw out the hook to catch it. The unfortunate boy tied the rope around his body and threw the hook out, but he missed, and the hook caught an ice floe that carried the boy with it. Two steps from the bank he was engulfed by huge chunks of ice. Everything just kept moving without the slightest pause.... There was no divine miracle. The village men couldn't do anything to help, and the mother stayed on the muddy riverbank crying desperately and tearing her clothes. Her face, like her bare breasts and her washerwoman's hands, was as white as molten metal. People looked away. Death and disaster are always naked, and people are too ashamed to look at them.

Boris, my dear, even spring here has begun to disgust me. It's not because of that boy; it's a general feeling. The sky is too thick and too empty; the water, impassable; the vegetation, scarce, and the people as Gorky described them. Cows wander through the village, as skinny as if they were in Biblical times, and they look out with the blank eyes of Greek statues. They eat the bark off the poplar stakes in the gardens and rub their shoulders on all the telegraph posts. The horses, who are enjoying a vacation before *they are sent off to work, walk over the mud on those wooden walkways, so it's the people who wind up walking in the mud. The young men sit on the piles of earth that reinforce the cabin walls and take a good look at the girls, who are dressed up in whatever they can buy at the local store. As a result, every other one is wearing a polka-dot dress; every third one is dressed in pink, and every fourth one is wearing a dress with a big floral print, which makes her look like a dappled mare. Every single one is wearing blue socks. There's a faint scent of cherries in the air that comes from the trees on the other side of the river, accompanied by the sound of a triumphant accordion, which is as schmaltzy as the cherries.*

The first boat came today. Some of the girls told me that not a single man on it was young and attractive. One young, well-dressed man did get off; however, since he has turned out to be an instructor for the regional committee of the Party, sent to supervise the ideological instruction of the organizations that make up the Komsomol, the interest he initially excited soon was replaced by fear.

Now we have sunlight twenty-four hours a day, but this hasn't made me feel any better.

{5}

While I'm waiting for Ella, my thoughts are with Ariadna: her rehabilitation in 1955. As soon as she reached Moscow, she began to collect her mother's poetry and correspondence for a first edition in the Soviet Union. Initially, she had nothing, no furniture, no cooking utensils, nothing. Marina's former room in the apartment she had shared with other inhabitants was completely empty, except for a trunk with her writings and a stuffed dog toy given to Ariadna by a friend to welcome her back to Moscow after her long absence.

On seeing how poor she was, Ariadna's friends brought her lots of stuff that wasn't always very useful. During the day, she earned a living by translating poetry. If it involved a language she didn't know (Spanish, German, Georgian, for example), she relied on a rough translation made by someone who was fluent. She wound up translating Baudelaire, Verlaine, Lope de Vega, and Goethe, to name a few. At night, she'd open the trunk that contained her mother's work, make clean copies of the poems, and organize the poetry as well as the correspondence.

Many people found her unfriendly and tactless. She would make harsh, unkind remarks directly to a person, but always deliver these judgments in a soft voice. "I say what I think, because I don't have time to make up lies," she'd insist.

Ariadna spent the last ten years of her life in Moscow. At the end of the 1950s, Pasternak invited her to share an apartment with his friend Olga Ivinskaya and her daughter Irina. In 1960, after the death of Pasternak, who had played the role of her father, brother, friend, and admirer, and after Olga and Irina had been arrested and sentenced to years in the Gulag—it was Olga's second time—Ariadna stayed in Moscow and dedicated her time to assembling Marina Tsvetaeva's archive, as well as writing her own work. Since she had a weak heart, she had a medical prescription allowing her to spend the

summers in Tarusa, outside the city. She finished several bi-
ographical works dedicated to her mother there, and it was
there, in 1975, that she died at sixty-three of a heart attack.

{6}

E lla comes with the tea and snacks and sits next to me on
the bed.

"Thanks for coming," she says in the sweet, little voice of
a child who's shy about speaking. But I sense that underneath
her delicate surface, Ella knows perfectly well what she wants.

"I'd like to hear your story," I suggest.

She starts to speak with enthusiasm.

"Three generations of my family suffered from retaliations.
It started before I was born, in 1924. At the beginning of the
1920s, my uncle and paternal grandfather were killed during
the sacking and destruction of the village church, which they
had tried to save, although they were Jewish. That happened
in Ukraine, during the civil war that followed the Revolution
and lasted five years, from 1917 to 1922. What happened to
my family was much like the atrocities Isaac Babel describes in
the stories in *Red Cavalry*.

"But the horror didn't end there. They took revenge on my
maternal grandmother: they arrested and killed her in 1926,
and in 1937 they arrested and shot my father.

"I was born in Tiflis, the capital of Georgia, which was
then one of the republics that formed the Soviet Union. There
were five in my family: my parents, my two sisters, and me.

My father was vice-minister of the Transcaucasian wood industry. Beria, the minister of Internal Affairs and a Georgian like Stalin, and my father hated each other, because my father had proposed a more equitable distribution of our resources between Georgia, which was rich in wood, and Armenia and Azerbaijan, which had almost none at all. Beria wanted it all for Georgia. They didn't take long to dismiss my father from his position and to give him a much more modest job as director of a construction consortium. Later he was accused of having misdirected the work of the consortium. With that excuse, they fired him again and made him director of a farming cooperative in Poti that produced mandarins.

"At one point, the president of the municipal committee of the Party called my father and asked why he didn't have a portrait of Beria in his office. My father tried to make a joke of it by saying that Beria had never given him one. Beria found out about it, and with sarcasm and spite he promised to give my father such a handsome portrait that he would admire it for the rest of his life. At the beginning of 1937, they arrested my father, and a little while later, they shot him.

"After my father's death, my mother undertook a sort of pilgrimage from one office to another, looking for work. They told her, 'Come back in a week. We'll see what we can do.' And when she went back, the people she had spoken to were no longer there; they had been arrested. Even people who lived with the illusion that they were safe, because they had an important position in the state hierarchy, were arrested and disappeared into the Gulag or were just shot. So many arrests.... It was like a tsunami, but long term. I don't understand how anyone failed to see what was being cooked up in the Communist Party."

{7}

They were going to send my sisters and me to an orphanage, but the administrators of the school where we were studying managed to put a stop to that. When they arrested my mother, they took us out of our apartment and sealed it off. We had a cat that was shut up in one of the rooms. She had no food, and she meowed nonstop. We tried to feed her by pushing food under the door, but it just didn't work. Then we went to the police station and begged them to free the animal. To our surprise, they actually did. To make up a little for our loss, they gave us a tiny apartment with two rooms.

"I was a good student at school. I was interested in science. Right before the war, I applied to study at the School of Mechanical Engineering and Math in Leningrad, but the Nazi invasion put an end to my plans.

"The German troops advanced at such a speed that by the end of August 1941, they occupied Donbass, the eastern side of Ukraine, where we were living. By that time, the NKVD had released my mother, so we lived together under the occupation. Before our village was liberated by Soviet troops in 1945, the region changed hands many times: the Nazis occupied it, the Soviets won it back, and so on until the end of the war.

"I remember clearly that during the war I wanted to fall into the Gestapo's hands, so they'd arrest me and let me show that I was a real Communist. Like many of my friends, I was convinced I had a vital mission of great historical importance: building communism. That's what we'd been taught since we were kids, and we believed it. That mission gave meaning to our lives and made us happy. The Soviet state encouraged activism and participation, especially in the political arena. The system depended on the interaction of people who would embody the messages that interested the state. We were used to being pro-Communist activists. We couldn't imagine any other way to think.

"What we learned in the 1920s and 1930s in the young Soviet Union under Stalin was that every one of our actions was incredibly important for the future. Anything we did might have a significance reaching beyond our own lives, beyond even the Soviet Union. The future was to be not just Soviet, but universal: with communism, happiness, equality for all.

"We—I'm talking about my generation—grew up totally convinced of the transcendence of everything we said and did. They taught us that our actions would decide, for better or worse, the future of the whole world. We heard that every day at every level of school. It was part of the air we breathed. All of us young people were filled with this sense of our own importance. You can't imagine how full and passionate life seems to someone who is convinced that she is helping build something great.

"Most people, even the young ones, believed in Stalin. He gave meaning to our little lives. But many others, the children of parents who had been victimized, were much more critical of him. We were the first dissidents. We believed in communism—we didn't reject it for a minute—but we believed in true communism, not in the communism practiced by Stalin and Beria, who used violence for their own ends.

"In both primary and secondary school we were taught to be ready at any time to sacrifice ourselves for the common good. As a result, when I turned nineteen, along with a few friends, we formed a terrorist organization that would make an attempt on the lives of Stalin and Beria, architects of the bloody dictatorship that had been established in the USSR. There were six of us: five boys and me. We called our group Death to Beria.

"We weren't naïve about our own shortcomings as assassins. We just wanted to make people aware of this political criminal who was decimating our country. Our major exploit was putting up proclamations inciting the public to wake up and see what was happening. We operated between 1943 and 1945, the year when we all moved to different locations. Our activities didn't cause us any problems until 1948, when a member of the group denounced us.

"We took such big risks in a regime that punished any deviation from established ideology, because we believed in our historic mission. Even though we knew we might be executed, we believed that future generations would see we were right and would honor us as heroes, as martyrs.

"I was the one who nourished a particular hatred for Beria, and—since I knew he was a hopeless womanizer—I decided to set a trap for him. I would seduce him—as a girl I was very good-looking—and then kill him. Just like Judith with Holofernes. He was disgusting, but I would have done it to wipe that mass murderer from the face of the earth. I would have executed him on behalf of my father, but not just for his sake, for the sake of the Russian people and of all humanity.

"Seeing yourself as a hero who sacrifices herself for the good of humanity produces a sort of sweet vertigo. It's like being drunk on your own importance. Perhaps Christ, as well as many other rebels, felt something like that.

"From our school days, we'd been trained to distinguish between good and evil. Our weapon was essentially criticism, and we formulated it very, very well. Mine was the first generation of young people who began to take a critical stance toward the Soviet Union, in spite of our great victory in the Second World War. After the war, not many of us sang odes in praise of the regime. Those days were over. One of my friends said that if somebody praised the USSR he was either an imbecile or a joker. That's what all of us believed. And furthermore, those of us who were Jews couldn't help noticing that we weren't treated as well as the gentiles.

"In our childhood universe, there were good people and bad people, and nobody in between, because—I'm repeating this because it's important for any understanding of the Soviet mentality—from the time we were small, they taught us that good and evil were separated by a very clear line. Our world was bipolar. The good people were Communists, the bad were capitalists, which is to say Westerners, and they were absolutely evil in the eyes of the regime, like anything else that might distract us from the construction of our Communist state. This division was basic, the essence of everything. So, from a young age, we were used to dividing the world and the people in it into good and bad, friends and enemies, saints and evildoers.

"We were taught to hate the evildoers. Yes, they taught us to hate, to denounce and to punish the bad people, especially the bad Communists who weren't sincere. From a young age, they taught us to hate. No one talked about love. What mattered was hatred. Punishing the evildoers was an essential part of the Soviet program for carrying out useful works.

"As I said, I was born in 1924, and my whole generation was like me, but not just my generation. Younger people were also burdened with the sense of a mission that had a historical importance. Parents even gave their children nicknames that referred to communism, that radiant aspiration. Lots of girls were called Lenina while boys were named Mels—for Marx, Engels, Lenin, and Stalin. Seven years after the Revolution, my parents, who were committed Communists, named me Kommunella, a name that didn't exist before the Revolution. I don't like this name anymore because of its connotations, so I use an abbreviated version: Ella. Most people felt proud of the Communist experiment. They saw it as sea of goodness that would eventually extend over the entire land, over the entire planet, over the entire universe."

{8}

But I was speaking of the Second World War, and I've digressed. One of my sharpest memories is of the day when the Soviets sent in a regiment of men by parachute to rescue our village from the Nazis. A fierce struggle ensued. The injured combatants were left in the street, and nobody helped them. I ran out and began dragging them to the village clinic, where I hoped to find some sort of medical assistance, but nobody was inside. I managed to get about seventy of them to a safe place. Then the Soviet hospital tent arrived. When they saw what I had done, they praised me and gave me a certificate attesting to my act of heroism so that I might be awarded a medal. But the Nazis didn't let up, and the Soviet troops finally took to their heels. We fell into the power of the Nazis once again. When the German soldiers saw a crowd of people in a combat zone, they killed all of them without batting an eye, riddling them with their machine guns. They were going to do the same thing to us, but I—who knew what they were like because we'd been occupied for two years— ran out to meet them and convinced them, using my German, that it was a civilian hospital.

"The Nazis kept guard at the doors of the clinic, keeping everyone inside, with the idea that the next day they'd identify who was there, because they suspected they were all Russians. Overnight, we managed to get the badly injured out through the emergency door and hide them in houses in the village. The next day, the Nazis discovered that the injured who had stayed in the clinic were Russian soldiers, so they arrested them all. Later they announced that anyone who was hiding a Soviet fighter at home would be shot, along with everybody else who lived on that street.

"During the Nazi occupation, there was a kind of employment exchange, where the German authorities provided identity cards to the residents. My friends talked me into working there so that I could get blank cards and then falsify them with the names of the injured who were hidden in the village. That way, if an injured soldier was discovered, they could show that he was a civilian who lived in the village. They contracted me as an interpreter, and I managed to get the cards that wound up saving many lives. When the Soviets finally liberated our village, they forbid everyone who'd lived under Nazi occupation from leaving home.

"My two sisters died in the siege of Leningrad. They could have been evacuated if they'd wished, but they refused since they wanted to keep on working in the hospital. That's what we Russians were like.

"I had lost a lot of time during the war, and I wanted to study at the university, so I asked for permission to leave the village. They investigated me and accused me of collaborating with the Nazis, because of my work in the employment exchange. My efforts to defend myself, along with the evidence I provided and that others provided as well, had no effect. Worse yet, as I've said, in 1948 a member of our terrorist group denounced all of us.

"They arrested us and, after half a year of investigation, condemned us to twenty-five years of forced labor. I didn't find out about the denunciation until the judicial hearing when I heard it from the informer himself, who publicly admitted to denouncing us. It didn't do him much good, since he got the same sentence as us. In fact, they sent him to the Karaganda camp in Kazakhstan, where the extreme weather conditions—in summer as well as winter—were far harder than the conditions in the north of Russia, inside the Arctic Circle, where the rest of our unfortunate group was sent.

"The truth is: the traitor had it worst of all since, once he'd started confessing, they demanded more and more information from him until he just didn't have any ink left in his bottle. This infuriated the investigators, who then accused him of a cover-up.

"Given the situation, we were lucky, since in 1947—exactly a year before our trial—the death penalty was abolished (they'd reinstate it in 1949). Besides, we all knew the risk we were taking when we formed a subversive organization, so we were mentally prepared to face prison and the rest of our punishment. That gave us strength during our sentences because, unlike many other prisoners, we knew why we were there. Before we were sent off to the camp, we swore to continue our struggle once we were free."

{9}

They condemned me to twenty-five years of forced labor in the mines of Vorkuta and Inta, beyond the Arctic Circle, with its unending ice. I stayed there until after Stalin had died. My other friends from the "Death to Beria" group had the same fate. After the war, the entire population of the territories that had been occupied by the Nazis was under suspicion. As the Soviets liberated Ukraine, the Baltic countries, Poland, and Germany, civilians from those areas began arriving in the camps. There were foreigners from all over.

People were dying like flies. In my case, the fact that I had lived in Ukraine compounded the fact that I'd created a terrorist group. It seemed like a cruel joke to be condemned to twenty-five years when it was hard to survive for even a couple of months.

"The one advantage of the rules of our sentence was our total separation, except in the places where we actually worked, from the common criminals, who were the political prisoners' worst enemies. They lived by their own code and never missed a chance to rob or kill anyone who did not form part of their band. When something like that happened, the authorities always looked the other way. According to the official Soviet ideology of the period, those common criminals were 'elements that are socially compatible with the regime.'

"The overwhelming majority of people who had recently been sent to the camps were young. Many were accused of separatist tendencies, especially the Ukrainians and the Baltic peoples, because there had been instances of armed resistance against the Bolsheviks in their countries. The same people who freed them from the Nazis subjugated them under the Soviet yoke."

{10}

I withstood life in the camp pretty well even though they gave me the hardest work: mining and road construction. I lived through a lot of very hard situations, but they toughened me up, and the variety of experiences I had to endure enriched me as a person. The thing is: the Gulag, just because it's so terrible, is also rewarding. That extreme suffering teaches you about yourself, about the people around you, and about human beings in general. I am grateful to the fate that sent me to the Gulag, because of everything I encountered and learned there.

"I learned, for example, that a person has to adapt to the situation, no matter what it is. Adaptability is the most important thing in life. Whoever couldn't get used to life in the camp was lost. The others swam on the surface, breathing easily, and wound up in control.

"When I was little, my father used to repeat an expression I've never forgotten: 'What are your enemies looking for? To see you frustrated, bitter, downcast. If you don't want to give your enemies that pleasure, then keep your head high.' And that's what I always did, especially in prison and in the camp. Thanks to this attitude, I can say that my time in the camp was worthwhile. I cannot imagine my life without this experience that made me strong and taught me what really matters.

"Being brave was essential to life in the Gulag. My mother, who had also learned something there, taught me that the person who gives in winds up dead. I remember that one time, while we were working, a prisoner approached one of the guards and asked if he couldn't have a little fun with one of the women prisoners. The guard said no and tried to throw the insolent guy out. The latter pulled out a knife and threatened the guard, who was already aiming his machine gun at the offender. Things were getting ugly, so I threw myself like a tigress against both of them and...disarmed them!

"Every day was a learning experience. In the camp I realized that the injustice I suffered was just part of the general tendency at that time. And not just that time. It was part of our system. Our system was based on injustice and capriciousness, and that was the system in which we believed, which we helped establish, which gave meaning to our lives, which filled our youth."

{11}

But now I'll tell you about something happier: the moment when I found out that Stalin had died. Do you want to hear? I had a friend at the camp, a professional painter who worked in the cultural-educational section, meaning she organized celebrations for the festival days on the Communist calendar: the Revolution, the First of May, that sort of thing. Her superiors had told her, confidentially, that Stalin was in very poor health. She thought about how to pass on that piece of wonderful news in such a way that I wouldn't get so excited I'd give myself away. Finally, after getting together with another friend of ours, she told me at the exact moment when I was taking off my felt boots after working all day. In an outburst of enthusiasm, I raised one of my boots high and shouted, 'Hurrah! Stalin is about to croak!' But he wasn't dead yet. When he finally died, we were working. Our guards in that camp, unlike others, were decent to us. They picked up our letters to be sent, and sometimes let us finish work before the official time. These guards said, 'Time to dance, girls! Stalin is dead!' On the other hand, the soldiers who guarded the men while they were at work got furious about Stalin's death and forced the prisoners to stand at attention in the intense cold of early March.

"My point here is that even our jailers were a varied lot. Merab Mamardashvili, the great Georgian philosopher, said that remaining human requires a constant effort. I often used to repeat that phrase to myself in the camp."

While we're drinking our second glass of tea, this time prepared by Ella's husband—an ex-prisoner she met in the camp, twenty years younger than his wife—she tells me that there's a poem she has remembered her whole life, a poem whose beauty helped her survive the camp conditions. She recites the verses with great emotion. I recognize stanzas from "Garden," by Marina Tsvetaeva:

Longing for homeland! Long ago
Exposed torment! To me
It is completely all the same
Where completely lonely to be,

By which stones on the road home
With the bazaar knapsack to drag
Home, not knowing, that it's mine,
Like hospital or a barrack.

It's the same to me, among which faces
Like an imprisoned lion to bristle,
And from among which people's midst
To be forced out—without fail—

Into oneself, into individual feelings.
As polar bear without ice floe
Where not to live—it's the same to me
(And I don't dare)—where to go low.

I won't be tempted by the milky
Call of the native tongue of my homeland.
It is the same to me on which
People would me misunderstand.

(To reader of newspaper tons,
To gulper, milker of rumors.) He
Is of the twentieth century,
And I—without a century!

Grown petrified just like a log
Remaining only of an alley,
They're all the same, it's all the same,
And maybe most the same—to me—

Dearer than everything that was.
All marks from me, all signs that were,
All dates—brushed off as if by hand:
Soul, that had once been born—somewhere.

Thus my land did not keep me there,
That the detective most keen
Along the soul, across it all!
The birthmark has not sought or seen!

Alien is home, temple—empty,
And all's the same and one to me.
But if along the road a bush
Rises, especially—ashberry . . .

{12}

When I say good-bye, I comment, "So, it was a joke when you told me that you don't read Marina Tsvetaeva."

The old woman hugs me and makes a face like a sphinx, without saying yes or no.

{13}

Ella Markman, who never stopped being animated and active, died a few months before I finished my book. She would have loved to see it published.

MINERVA IN THE MINES

Elena Korybut-Daszkiewicz

{1}

E lena Korybut-Daszkiewicz greets me with the simplic-
ity and composure of someone accustomed to receiving
guests of a certain class. Even though her home is situated in
the midst of the tedium and ugliness of the *khrushchevki* com-
plexes, it feels elegant, and it is furnished with antiques from
Central Europe. Korybut-Daszkiewicz—who uses her married name, Markova, for her scientific work—serves me tea in
a set of Sèvres porcelain, surely one of the relics she managed
to recover from the wars and revolutions that menaced the
home she grew up in as part of the Polish aristocracy.

It takes me a while to notice that, like other women who
have been in the Gulag, Elena has a hard time walking or
standing up for very long, a problem caused by prolonged
malnutrition, but she is gracious and dignified. Before asking
me to sit in one of the armchairs, she shows me her prodigious

archive on the Gulag. Here she has gathered together books, letters, documents, photographs, and drawings.

Both warm and professional, Elena encourages me to ask questions: "I want everything to be known, both here and in the West. Ask me whatever you like. I'll tell you everything. I'm a compendium, an encyclopedia of the Gulag."

While she is telling her story, our cups clink against the saucers. The tea is delicious. Her daughter, Inna, who is about fifty and has a young face, refills the beautiful little teapot more than once. Every time she comes back into the dining room, she casts a loving look at her mother.

Elena starts her narration, keeping it concise and emphasizing with great precision the details that will give it the meaning it deserves.

{2}

The liberators, which is to say the Soviets, arrested us during the Second World War, after the Battle of Stalingrad in 1943. They had decided that the entire population of the territories under Nazi occupation were collaborators and traitors. Many of us who wound up in the Gulag were Ukrainians; others were from the Baltic republics, from the eastern part of Poland or from Belarus, in addition to numerous Russian Jews, who were victims of Stalin's anti-Semitism.

"My father, who was a teacher, had been arrested during the purges of 1937 and shot shortly after that. His death left my mother and me in poverty. My mother, Wacława

Korybut-Daszkiewicz, was from an old, aristocratic Polish family. She had studied math, foreign languages, and music at the University of Kiev, the city where I was born in 1923.

"We spent the war in Donbass, in Ukraine. During that time, I worked in the hospital, which passed back and forth between Russian and German hands repeatedly, according to the fortunes of war. I worked as a nurse trying to help the injured soldiers no matter which side they were on. Since I spoke fluent German, when the Nazis were in charge of the hospital, I often acted as interpreter between the Russian wounded and the health directors. When the German armies beat their last retreat, before leaving our city, Krasnoarmiisk—which was called Grishino at some points and now is known as Pokrovsk—they burned down a lot of houses, along with the jail. All the prisoners died in the blaze. I imagine that if they had had more time, the Nazis would have set the hospital on fire as well."

{3}

When the German troops withdrew from the territories they had occupied, including Krasnoarmiisk, my sole thought was to enroll in the university. To do that, I asked for permission to move to Leningrad. But, instead of helping me, the workers who processed the transfers accused me of collaboration and arrested me. Since the jail had burned down, they sent me to a temporary detention center.

"This was an enormous, dark, underground hole, like a huge tomb, that was crammed with people. There were no bathrooms, no water for washing. People did their business wherever they could. The hole was sealed hermetically so that there was virtually no air to breathe; people got sick; they fainted, and the old ones died. We were given very little food and, worse yet, almost no water. We were in darkness night and day.

"But, once we got used to the constant twilight, we could make out the faces of our companions in misfortune, and we tried to establish contact with them. People used their eyes to communicate with one another. There were instances of friendship or even love. Many of us survived thanks to those silent communications. In extreme conditions like that, one man can annihilate another with a single gesture or save his life just by giving him a kind look. I know, because I witnessed it."

{4}

After a few weeks, they transported me to the city of Stalino, now Donetsk, in Ukraine. During the investigation of my case, with its corresponding interrogations, I thought about my family's destiny. I was part of the third generation of prisoners. At the end of the 1920s, my grandfather, Michal Korybut-Daszkiewicz, died of a heart attack during an interrogation in the prison at Kiev. My father was arrested in 1937, and they put him in the same prison. Soon after, they sent my mother, another Korybut-Daszkiewicz, to the same place. Six years later, I was the one in prison. They accused me of collaborating with the Nazis and condemned me to fifteen years of forced labor—the hardest punishment on the scale—for betraying my country."

{5}

In June 1944, after a long journey from Stalino, the prisoners got out at the Kotlas camp. They had transported us on a cargo ship down the Dvina River. We got there very late, but, since it was the season of the white nights, we could see everything as though it were daytime. On one bank of the wide river we could make out a green landscape of woods and hills, with a white church that had gilded cupolas. On the other bank were long, dark barracks. These were two very different worlds. I felt as though I were seeing it from the River Lethe: the dark bank, high and hard to reach, led to hell; the other, luminous and lovely, was the entrance to paradise.

"Before going to bed, in the barracks where they gave us a nasty concoction for supper, I sat next to an old man with a white beard. He was a Siberian, and it turned out that he was in prison for practicing shamanism, which was forbidden. He asked me to show him the palm of my hand. I had never liked having my future told, but I didn't want to offend him, and besides I was curious.

"'Your journey will be long and hard,' he told me. 'Many setbacks lie ahead of you, and you'll often find yourself in tight spots. You'll feel death at your heels more than once. There will be moments that are so terrible that you wish yourself dead. You will lose your long blonde hair, and they will shut you up under the earth.'

"I trembled, and he realized he was upsetting me: 'But don't ever be afraid. Never! That's the important thing. You will overcome it all, but you won't be able to go home for many years. Once you've been liberated, you will experience happiness and success. I see books. You will be the one who writes them, and you will become well-known and distinguished. You won't die until you're very old, and you'll be surrounded by members of your family.'

"The next day, they took us farther north."

{6}

When we reached the camp where we were to stay, I came down with erysipelas, but it healed in a couple of weeks. Anya, my doctor, kept me on in the clinic as her assistant. So, the first work they gave me at the camp was as a nurse. I was familiar with that profession because, as I told you before, I had worked as a nurse in my city during the war and the Nazi occupation.

"One day, Anya told me, 'Let's hope Buydan likes you.'

"I didn't understand why somebody had to like me, but I just asked, 'Who is Buydan?'

"'He's the director of the clinic.'

"At last, Buydan gave his approval for me to keep working there. They gave me the night shift. I was the only nurse on duty, and there were deaths every night. I was on my own with the dying, with their complaints and their tears. I couldn't help them or even alleviate their pain, because we had almost no medicine and the sanitary conditions were deplorable. The most common illness was dystrophy. I had seen it when I was working as a nurse during the war, but back then people were dying for their country, and this certainty made them feel better. Here they were dying from starvation and from the inhuman conditions. Most of them would have lived if they'd been fed enough, but they were just skin and bones. The bunks were filled with living skeletons covered with skin. I still looked normal, because I had just reached the camp. I was almost ashamed of my good health, my youth, and because I looked like a human being.

"One day I noticed that Anya was wearing a dress under her lab coat; they didn't force her to wear a prisoner's rags. More than that, she had pretty hair, unlike the new arrivals. Before they even let us in the camp, while we stood outside in the snow, a crew of men cut off all our hair—even our pubic hair—with just a few slashes. They didn't even look at us.

"Anya's blonde hair, which had been shaved off too, had had time to grow enough to form a cute little boy's hairdo. It looked as though she had chosen that cut on purpose because it was so becoming. Her black dress emphasized her slim figure. The power of clothes! Amid prisoners who were wearing dirty, half-torn work gear, Anya seemed like a girl sitting in an expensive restaurant, waiting for an elegant man who would turn up at any minute. However, in reality, the only man who would turn up for her was a disheveled prisoner, dressed in filthy, stinking rags. Wearing work clothes was part of our punishment; it was yet another way to humiliate, demoralize, and control us.

"One time, during my night shift, a man came in and started shouting, 'This is a pigsty!'

"Then he walked between the bunks where the patients lay, still shouting nonsense. He asked me about the serious cases, and I told him that a few people had just died. He blamed me for the deaths and carried on so that I thought he'd have a heart attack.

"The next day, I told Anya; the girl laughed, 'That's Buydan's tactic. He wants to scare you so that later it will be easier for him to take advantage of you.'

"'I want to leave this job,' I said, indignant. 'I'm not here so that somebody can take advantage of me.'

"'You don't seem to realize where you are, sweetie. You're a nobody here, and you don't have a choice. In this camp, there are lots of men and very few women. There are other camps just for women, but here you have to get used to men looking at you. And it won't stop at furtive glances and gentlemanly propositions. We have no rights. Nobody will pay attention to our complaints. Most people here are totally dehumanized. You have to survive; it's the only thing that matters. And just so you realize, the director of this clinic is not the worst choice. You could wind up in the claws of the common criminals, the thieves and murderers.'

"'The thieves and murderers are in here with us? They haven't separated them?'

"'You'd work in the mines with them. Most of the women who get sent there are prostitutes. Right away, somebody would take hold of you and make you his property. If you protest, they'll kill you or mutilate you, which is just as bad. I would advise you not to reject Buydan's propositions, but if you're a holy virgin or if you just can't stand Buydan, then remember that it's forbidden to use violence—although everyone does. Since he is about to be freed (he was sentenced in 1937), maybe he'll want to avoid problems and won't force you.'"

{7}

The next day, I asked them to send me to the mines. I knew that would be the end of my career in medicine, helping the sick in a relatively warm building, my dream of wearing decent clothes instead of the prisoners' repugnant rags, and yet I felt as though I'd won. I'm going to work in the mines, I thought, but worse than the mines would be losing my sense of self.

"During the long years of my imprisonment, I saw a few cases of women defending their honor. That may seem unlikely: We were just slaves, less than slaves. We had absolutely no rights at all. But when that happened, it was usually thanks to the woman's strong will.

"After I left the clinic, Anya fell in love. She had a boyfriend in spite of all the prohibitions, warnings, and threats. Their love lasted for the rest of the time they were imprisoned. She became pregnant once, and, since she knew that the authorities were obliged to separate babies from their mothers, she chose to have an abortion. In the primitive conditions of the clinic, they botched the job, and Anya was near death. At that time, Buydan was no longer there, so I went back to working as a nurse. I was on duty while Anya was critically ill from septicemia. Even though I covered her up with everything I could find, she couldn't stop trembling like an epileptic, but she recovered. The next time she got pregnant, she decided to have the baby. She gave birth to a little girl. That's how Anya started a family in the Gulag."

{8}

Since I'd rejected my boss—Buydan—and with him, a tolerable life working in the clinic, I got to know what life was like for a normal prisoner in the mines of Vorkuta. No hygiene, a superhuman work load, malnutrition: all of these things transformed the inmates into dying invalids who almost all perished a few months after reaching the camp. Many of them died in the mines because of the daily accidents. Workplace safety and mechanization were notable only for their complete absence. No one got even the most elemental instruction in mining, which demands special knowledge and practices. It was all kept very simple: the same day a new group of prisoners arrived, they were sent to work underground, women as well as men. They were new; they were fresh and therefore of some use.

"I'll never forget my first day in the mine. It was Number 9. The guards led us up to the dark entrance. On top of our overcoats, they attached miners' lamps that ran on kerosene.

Their yellowish, intermittent glow did nothing to light our way. They pushed us, one by one, down the hole. We descended, practically feeling our way, along a narrow, sloping tunnel, sinking into holes and bumping against obstacles that were impossible to identify. Streams of water fell from the roof onto our heads. The ground was slippery. Every once in a while, somebody fell, the ones coming behind piled up on top of him, the lights went out. . . . At last we reached the gallery. Once we were there, the men would tear out the coal, and the women would load it. My first job was to shovel the coal that had been extracted. The blaster (a free man who was contracted to do the work; the prisoners were not allowed to handle explosives) would set up the fuses and light them so the rock exploded. Then the men would load the coal that had come loose onto toboggans, and the women had to shovel the chunks together. I usually could not manage that much work. The coal piled up fast, threatening to close off the gallery and bury me under its weight. Then the foreman (one of the common prisoners) came running, spitting out insults the whole time, to give me a beating, but since laying into me didn't reduce the volume of coal that was piling up at a terrifying rate, he himself would have to clear the passageway.

"At the end of a few days of work in the mine, I began to count on the unexpected help of the blaster, who took pity on me and would lend me a hand when the coal started to pile up. I didn't know much about him, since he almost never spoke to me. (The contracted workers were forbidden to speak to the prisoners.) He was named Volodia, and he was from Leningrad. After he'd finished his degree as a mining engineer, they sent him to Vorkuta. He was moved by the situation of the prisoners and the very existence of forced labor in our country. While he shoveled the coal to help me, he asked me a few questions. First of all, he wanted to know why I was there. I told him as briefly as I could the story of the hospital. Sometimes Volodia brought me food, and, for New Year in 1945, he gave me a present: a sewing needle and a bobbin of thread. We weren't allowed to have things like that to mend our clothes, so we were forced to wear rags. Someone told on him, however, and they moved him to another mine."

{9}

Many of the prisoners were killed by extrajudicial executions. The most common pretext was attempted escape. When we went to or from work, we always had an escort. The order was clear: 'Left, right, left.... Anything else will look like an attempt to escape, and the escort will shoot without warning.' Exhausted people, incapable of walking in a straight line, might stumble or wobble or get left behind. They were shot immediately, in front of everybody. The same thing happened to those who got too close to the 'forbidden zone': a border of loose earth between the high outer wall and the inner barbed-wire fence. An 'attempt to escape' served as an excuse for anything. In the forced labor camps, there was no end to the abuse. In the summer, if a prisoner committed a small offense, he was left naked to the waist and forced to stand next to the watchtower. The mosquitoes ate him alive.

It was impossible to stay still. With the first movement, a shot would ring out....

"Mass executions were frequent. In the late 1940s, in Mulda, the entire population of a men's Gulag was massacred on the pretext of a 'protest.' The floors and walls of the barracks in that razed camp were still spotted with blood and fragments of human brains when our group of prisoners was sent there to replace the victims....

"In March 1946, nine men from the Baltic republics took flight. The guards caught them and had the dogs tear them apart. Their cadavers were exhibited on the snow at the entrance of the camp as a warning. They put noticeboards by them with the warning, written in blood: 'A dog's death to the dogs!' It wasn't the first time they had practiced these sinister 'exhibitions.' It had already happened in Mine 9.... Of the fugitives, I only knew one by name. He was called Neeneh.

"People from the Baltic republics had begun to show up at the camp at the end of 1945, but the majority of them didn't reach us until 1946. One load of prisoners after another arrived from Lithuania, Latvia, and Estonia. Waiting for the gates of hell to open, the band whose turn it was would stand at the entrance of the Gulag, where they could be seen clearly from the women's sector, which was located on slightly higher ground. We, 'the class of 1943,' looked in surprise at these young 'brothers from the woods,' as they used to call the Baltic guerrillas who still had the strength and energy to fight against Soviet power. They were wearing beautiful, warm clothes, cut in a Western style. My god! It was incredible that well-dressed, human-looking people still existed! They looked as though they had come from another world, a fantastic world. After two years in the camp, we looked like all the other prisoners: with dirty, torn jackets, pants lined with cotton, a kind of laced boot made of felt and caps with flaps to cover our ears. We all looked as though we'd been cut out of the same pattern. We could only be distinguished by the numbers that were painted on our clothes. A few months later, not a trace remained of the human appearance of the new arrivals. Their pretty clothes had disappeared; the thick wool jerseys had been replaced by torn jackets. With an amazing speed, the exhausting labor and the swill that all the prisoners ate had transformed the strong, healthy young men into half-dead invalids. The forced labor camps were extermination camps. It's not for nothing that they were called 'forced labor camps with a particularly harsh regimen for traitors to their country.'"

{10}

To keep from falling into despair, while I worked in the mine, I recalled poems that I knew from memory and recited them to myself in a whisper, or I sang in a low voice arias that I knew from my mother's repertoire. One day, a barracks mate from Latvia recognized an aria from *The Gold of the Rhine*, and she told me that Wagner had started composing that opera in Riga. Once we were in the barracks for the night, we started to talk about Wagner and his concept of the total work of art, the *Gesamtkunstwerk*. We searched our memories for all of Wagner's operas. I pronounced their names in the original German, especially his last one, *Der Fliegende Holländer*. My companion understood what I was saying, because in Latvia the operas were sung in German, unlike Russia, where they were translated. Then we started talking about the friendship between Wagner and Liszt and his daughter, Cosima, who married Wagner.

"After this conversation, I couldn't sleep for a long time because I kept hearing Wagner's melodies. That night I felt like a human being again.

"The next day, to my surprise, I was told to go see a supervisor. It didn't even occur to me that it was because of the conversation about Wagner's operas. But my words had been twisted around! The supervisor formulated a sinister accusation. According to him, I was guilty of supporting racism, the fascist ideology, of glorifying Nazi statesmen and other things along those lines. The names of German composers had been changed into the names of Nazi higher-ups. The supervisor's office became the setting for a scene from the theater of the absurd! Dramas like that were very familiar to me after having endured the investigation into my case. The supervisor had his own version of what I had talked about with the Latvian the previous night in the barracks, and it had nothing to do with music or composers. In his version, historical events from the nineteenth century were transposed to the present day, and the names of German composers were supplanted by those of famous Nazis. The supervisor insisted I admit 'quite frankly' that I had praised those Nazis. I refused and explained repeatedly the plot of the opera to show what had really happened.

"'Why on earth did you start a conversation about composers? Are you a professional musician? I have your information here. You were sent to the camp when you were in your last year of secondary school, isn't that right? In Soviet schools, nobody studies German composers. You're lying. You two weren't talking about composers. You were talking about Fascists!'

"I had to spend a lot of time showing him his version was mistaken and explaining why I had started talking about composers.

"'Although I'm not a professional musician, I was educated in a family of music lovers. My mother and my grandmother studied in the conservatory. You could always hear music and singing in our house. I read about Wagner when I was still a child; that's why I know his music even though I didn't study it in school.'

"The supervisor did not want to give in, and he interrogated me at great length about my mother's and grandmother's studies, hoping to catch me in a lie. He was delighted when I said that my grandmother had studied in the conservatory in Warsaw!

"'So, it turns out that your grandmother lived abroad so you, even before you were born, had a propensity for the West.'

"'My grandmother studied in Warsaw at the end of the last century when Warsaw and almost all Poland were part of Russia.'

"That was the nature of my visits to the supervisor's office. That time, he had me shut up in solitary confinement to separate me from my friends in the barracks on the pretext of keeping me from influencing possible witnesses. Later, almost all of them were interrogated about it by the supervisor. Most of them hadn't even heard or had only the barest idea of that conversation. And those who had still couldn't give any specifics. But that didn't bother the supervisor, since he wasn't trying to get to the truth, but rather to back up his thesis. Any possible witness was urged to 'collaborate with the investigation' in order to show her own value as a Soviet citizen and to show that she was vigilant about subversion. If she didn't, she'd be considered an accomplice of fascism. Given such a situation, there were women who were willing to testify to anything.

"During those days, my future depended entirely on what the witnesses would say. If one or two people confirmed the supervisor's version, I might be given an additional sentence. And since I'd been sentenced to fifteen years of forced labor, a new sentence would have no point. Instead, I'd be sentenced— and this was habitual—to being shot for 'fascist propaganda.'

"I don't know how my statement was verified. Someone must have recognized the names of German composers and of Wagner's works, and that saved my life. My only punishment was being shut up in a solitary cell."

{11}

After months of ice and snow and temperatures that hovered around fifty degrees below zero, in August we'd be blessed at times with a few warm days. I remember that in the first week of August 1947, it really felt like summer. At about that time, I went back to taking the night shift in the clinic. When I returned to the barracks at nine in the morning and the sun was shining, I felt as though I had wings.

"I told myself that I had to seize the moment, and one day I stopped to look at the sunny tundra, an image I could very seldom enjoy. I looked over the immense space that was almost green and then raised my eyes to the sky. Like the steppes, there were no mountains or even rolling hills here to block my view of the horizon. Yet oddly, even as I took it in, I sensed that the tundra wasn't green and friendly, but instead gray and heartless, and that its embrace wasn't like a mother's, but a stepmother's. A chill ran over me.

"To escape from these contradictory sensations, I lay down by the barracks on top of a blanket. It was critical to enjoy whatever pleasant moments we could, so we'd have the will to keep going in spite of everything. The sun warmed me, and I felt like a child on a beach by the sea during my vacation. Lying on top of a blanket, I looked at the sky, which usually seemed to be weighed down by clouds and mist. Seeing the high, blue heavens made me feel as if I were in the south. That is, until my barracks mate Valentina Mikhailovna came over. Her voice shattered my happy, luminous meditation.

"'Oh, you crazy little thing!' she said. 'Why are you lying down in the mud? You're going to get sciatica and pneumonia!'

"'What I'm getting is intense pleasure from the sunlight and the warmth. Come here, and I'll tell you a story about Chopin.'

"'I'm not going to encourage this silliness.'

"After an hour, Valentina came back to tell me if I kept on like that I'd have a sunstroke. I laughed.

"'It's better to die sunbathing than to live in the middle of the clouds.'

"That day, instead of sleeping in the barracks, I stayed outside sunbathing. Before heading to the clinic, I had the joy of seeing a crimson sunset."

{12}

What was the hardest work of all?" I ask Elena. "Could anything be worse than spending days and nights in total darkness and without food in an icy solitary cell and then having to go out to work in the mines or on a railroad track?"

"Yes," she answers. "I had an experience that was crueler, in a more refined way. In the depths of winter, when there is never any light and the sun doesn't appear for even a moment, they sent me and other prisoners to build a wall with stones so heavy we could hardly lift them. One day they forced us to build it, and the next day, they ordered us to tear it down. That happened day after day. The worst torture of all was the futility of a superhuman effort."

{13}

What saved me in large part was beauty," Elena affirms. "When I could, I'd write a sort of diary, even though

any writing at all was strictly forbidden. The tundra, the habi-
tat in which we lived, was a landscape that I came to both love
and hate, and I often wrote about these feelings."

{14}

E lena has taken out one of her diaries and read aloud from
it: a prose poem about the landscape around the camp.
Afterwards, while she is putting her notebook away, I ask her
a number of questions. The old woman comes back and sits
down comfortably. After sipping her tea and replacing the cup
in the saucer, she considers her experience:

"I realize that some of my campmates argue that their lives
would not be so full without the experience of the Gulag.
I disagree. If I could live my life over, I would like to have
started in the university at eighteen and, after finishing my
studies, dedicated myself to my work in full. The Gulag was
a waste of time, of health, of energy. Human beings are made
to search for happiness and beauty, to do something that is
fulfilling. To say the experience of the Gulag is essential to
learning about life just seems perverse, even though I understand why they say that: my companions miss the friendships
that became so close in the Gulag. However, when you live
in freedom, you can also form great friendships. I believe that
the positive effects of life in the Gulag do not compensate for
everything that is negative about it. In my experience, nothing
made the Gulag worthwhile. My only happy memory of the
camps is tied to the theme of books."

Elena shows me a book by Pushkin, interspersed with old engravings, published in 1905. "In the camp, this book of unknown origin passed through hundreds, maybe even thousands of hands. Books have their own lives, their histories and their ends, just as men do."

Then she shows me an archive of letters that some prisoners—philosophers and writers—sent her secretly from one barracks to another. With the greatest care, I touch those little pieces of paper covered with a minuscule, faded handwriting and see that they speak of Kierkegaard, Goethe, Beethoven, Gogol. . . .

{15}

"Everything I achieved later in life I owe to the few books that I managed to read in the Gulag," she concludes and then exclaims, "No one can imagine what a book meant to the prisoners: it was salvation! Beauty, liberty, and civilization in the midst of total barbarity!

"Oddly enough, my life developed exactly along the lines that the ancient shaman had predicted. After Stalin's death in 1953, and thanks to my mother's heroic efforts, the new authorities reduced my sentence to a kind of provisional freedom. I felt terribly let down because, even though I left the Gulag, I was forced to live in the same area, in Vorkuta. The worst part is that I wasn't allowed to register in the university, which is what mattered most to me. I had no work and no money.

"At last, thanks to the intervention of friends, I found work in a chemical laboratory in the city. It was there, in Vorkuta, that I married another ex-prisoner. My husband, a man of great humanity with a highly developed sense of ethics, worked as the director of the theater in Vorkuta. In 1954, I was given permission to enroll in correspondence courses at the Polytechnic University of Vorkuta. In 1960, when I moved to Moscow with my husband and my three-year-old daughter Inna, I had a diploma that made it possible for me to study in the Institute of Automatization and Cybernetics. I was thirty-seven years old.

"When I got to the capital, I was confronted with an easygoing lifestyle that was very different from what I had known in Vorkuta, which had become a refuge for prisoners or ex-prisoners of the Gulag. I had to adapt to this new mentality, but I never got used to its superficiality. People complained about insignificant things and led shallow lives without really giving any thought to what mattered.

"I think the Gulag helped me find a sense of values, to distinguish between what was meaningful and what was trivial. I focused on my studies and, later, on my work, taking advantage of every minute, almost every second, to do something worthwhile. If I was traveling by metro, for example, I always carried a book of art or philosophy or, especially, the classics—whether they were Russian or universal—and I took advantage of the time to read and to learn. I didn't go to cafes or restaurants with my friends. I preferred to dedicate all my time to my work.

"I became a specialist in cybernetics and computer technology. I published a number of books in that area and participated in many international conferences in the Western capitals as one of the few women in that field. I didn't retire until I was eighty, but I keep writing scientific articles as well as texts about my experiences in the Gulag. I want to die as a person whose merits have been recognized . . . and surrounded by my family!"

1. Zayara at the time of her arrest.

2. Nikolai Biletov, the violinist.

3. Natasha Geister, Zayara's fellow prisoner.

4. Village of Pikhtovka, drawn by Nikolai Biletov.

5. ". . . when I come out of the subway, I feel as though I'm in a different country, one that has nothing to do with downtown Moscow. I'm surrounded by gaudy signs for stores and movie theaters as well as stands selling fruit or food from Russia's Asian republics. I'm on a wide avenue, built during Khrushchev's administration, and I feel as if I were in Russian Asia during the Communist years."

6. "The geraniums, which are in flower, are arranged carefully to hide at least part of the sixth-floor view of an interminable line of buildings made from prefabricated panels. The Russians call these apartments *khrushchevki*, because they were part of Khrushchev's plan to make Moscow grow."

7. Zayara Vesiolaya and her husband.

8. "... the inmates in the collective cells at Lubyanka Prison opened their mouths and rubbed their eyes when I appeared in the doorway, a seventeen-year-old with braids, wearing a carefully ironed child's dress with a white collar."

9. Susanna Pechuro on her release from the Gulag, in 1956.

10. Boris Slutsky.

11–12. Lina Prokofiev, before and during the Gulag.

13. Susanna Pechuro in 2008.

14. "The front door of the apartment is open, just as Susanna Pechuro had told me it would be when we spoke earlier on the phone."

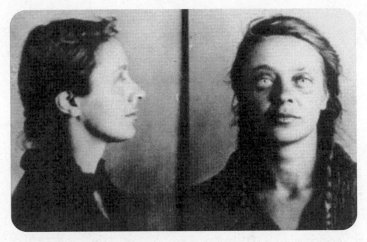

15. Ariadna Efron, daughter of Marina Tsvetaeva, in the Gulag.

16. Ella Markman in her Moscow apartment in 2013.

17. Elena in 1943.

18. "It takes me a while to notice that, like other women who have been in the Gulag, Elena has a hard time walking or standing up for very long, a problem caused by prolonged malnutrition . . ."

19–20. "It all began during the Second World War, in 1944, when I met Bill," Valentina tells me almost eagerly. "We danced together at the International Club of Arkhangelsk, which was frequented by US marines and English soldiers."

21. Valentina, in one of the performances in the Gulag.

22. "Tatiana was a big draw, of course. All the prisoners had seen her films, and her presence lent a special glow to our performances."

23. "Finally, a woman at a construction site tells me where the right street is and I find Valentina. She is an old woman in a wheelchair, who has apparently just gotten up. Her apartment is nearly empty."

NATALIA GORBANEVSKAYA

24. Natalia Gorbanevskaya in the 1960s.

25. "We sit at a little table spread with books and papers, overflowing ashtrays, plates and cups—a Meissen set—with what's left from breakfast."

26. The London neighborhood where Janina currently lives.

27. ". . . her thoughts have wandered far from the apartment in the south of London where I am paying her a visit and where we have settled down in a sitting room decorated with dolls whose eyes open and close, paper flowers, photographs, and souvenirs of all sorts."

GALYA SAFONOVA

28. Galya as a university student.

29. Galya Safonova today.

30. From left to right: Olga Ivinskaya, Boris Pasternak, and Irina Emelyanova in 1959.

31. Irina, Georges Nivat, and Vadim Kozovoi.

32–33. "Vadim gave Irina his diary to read. She shows it to me. The entries are long and written in a minuscule handwriting to take advantage of all the space in the notebook, since any kind of paper was very hard to come by in the camps."

34. "Elena shows me a book by Pushkin, interspersed with old engravings, published in 1905. 'In the camp, this book of unknown origin passed through hundreds, maybe even thousands of hands. Books have their own lives, their histories and their ends, just as men do.'"

PSYCHE IN PRISON

Valentina Iyevleva

{1}

Valentina is one of the last women I visit in Moscow. By this point I have done several interviews with women who had survived the Gulag and after every story I'd heard, I spent a sleepless night. I feel exhausted. I get up very early, because I have to catch the metro to the outskirts of the city and then a commuter train that passes infrequently and irregularly, with no fixed schedule, to reach the suburb where Valentina lives. It feels as though I will never reach Shcherbinka and I feel like giving up. I sit on one of the benches in the park that surrounds the Tsaritsyno Palace and call Valentina to tell her that I am canceling the appointment.

"But dear, tell me why. Why ever not?"

"I can't reach your house. There's no train."

"You're a writer, aren't you?"

"I try to be."

"And you want to write a book?"

"Yes."

"And do you think this book will just fall into your hands? That it will write itself? Look, dear, when you really want something, you have to go after it. Go all out for it! Otherwise, you'll never do anything worthwhile in life. If the first obstacle stops you from coming to visit me, it's better to stay at home and not to do anything."

With my head down, ashamed, I wait more than two hours on a platform swept by the humid, autumn wind, with wintertime temperatures, to get on the first train for Shcherbinka. It turns out that they didn't give me the ticket I asked for at the ticket window, and my journey ends one stop too soon. An irritated ticket collector fusses at me, but with a tired gesture lets me continue. Once I'm in Shcherbinka I spend a long time looking for the right street and the right house, since this suburb is still being built and the houses are not yet numbered. Natives of Kyrgyzstan, Uzbekistan, and Chechnya follow me in their cars, watching me with their dark gazes, advancing on me as I walk. But I would not dream of giving up.

Finally, a woman at a construction site tells me where the right street is and I find Valentina. She is an old woman in a wheelchair, who has apparently just gotten up. Her apartment is nearly empty. I wonder why.

"I never had anything, just books. I was always a great reader, but my children did not let me bring my books here, just three or four. They say books don't have a future."

She makes me go into the kitchen, the only room in the apartment that gives evidence of life. We sit at the table, which is covered with teabags, a kettle, and a few boxes of cookies. I listen to her story there.

{2}

"It all began during the Second World War, in 1944, when I met Bill," Valentina tells me almost eagerly. "We danced together at the International Club of Arkhangelsk, which was frequented by US marines and English soldiers. Bill was an American, one of those who brought the Soviet Union help— food, but also ammunition and arms—on his ship, the *Thomas Hardy*. Bill was my great love; I got pregnant with his child, and months after he left our city, I gave birth to Bella. I called her Bella, because it sounds like Bill in a feminine form. He knew nothing about it. He never found out that he had a daughter in Russia or that they had shut his girlfriend up in the Gulag for having known him."

"You never communicated with each other again?" I ask her in amazement.

"No. I think he tried to get in touch, since some signs of his efforts reached me. If it fits into my story, I'll get to it later," she adds a bit impatiently. "So, after the war, I was a very young mother and a drama student."

"You must have been about twenty, weren't you? Or a little older?"

"I wasn't twenty yet," she answers, a little irked by my interruptions.

My questions obviously put her off, so I tell myself to keep quiet. After sorting through her memories for a moment, Valentina takes up her story again.

"It happened a few years after the war had ended. One night when I had just fallen asleep with Bella in my arms—she was two then—and my mother was sleeping in the kitchen, I was awakened by the bell and knocks and kicks at the door. At that point, the light was suddenly turned on, and three strangers—two men and an older woman—burst into my room. They took me to the prison. From there, after some time I was sent then to the camp."

Valentina looks to see if the water is boiling. She puts a couple of bags of Earl Grey into a white teapot and pours the boiling water over them. I get ready to pour the tea, but Valentina suggests that we let it sit a little longer.

After a bit, after it's poured, she starts sipping her tea while she looks through the kitchen window. She points out the snowflakes that are floating in the air. Then she clears her throat and takes up her story again.

"At the camp every night, before the morning's reveille, I dreamed about my mother and my daughter. The dream was always the same: the three of us were going back home and, before we got there, my mother and Bella disappeared. I looked for them in vain, and that just undid me. I woke up every morning feeling terribly upset and frustrated.

"One night, while I was having my soup in the canteen, I told an old Siberian about it; he was imprisoned for being a shaman. Without hesitating, he told me that it was a sign that something in my life would change soon.

"I told the shaman how unhappy I was—I who had never done anything bad—at being so far away from my loved ones.

"'You mustn't look at it that way. They have imprisoned you unjustly; that's your advantage. You didn't do anything, so morally you're stronger than the other ones!'

"'But living in this filthy hole...'

"'Make an effort to ignore the filth. When spring comes, look at the shining snow, the blue sky, the contrast between light and darkness, which is enormous here. Now that it's winter and the sun doesn't come out, concentrate on the different shades of gray: some are blue gray; other are almost rose-colored. Don't forget to look at the barbed wire and our pathetic huts as if you were taking a photograph, looking for the right shot. You'll see that even in the midst of ugliness, it's possible to find beauty.'

"'And what can you tell me about the barbarity and the evil?'

"'Take pity on the evildoers; they are bad because they are weak. Find friends like yourself, and those friendships will last you through life. It's what always happens in the middle of unhappiness.'"

{3}

One day I was taken into the NKVD office of the camp to identify a cadaver. They wanted me to say it was a certain Fyodor Ivanovich Punin, but I couldn't possibly have recognized that person since his face was completely destroyed and covered with blood. The guards had probably beaten him with the butts of their guns or his fellow prisoners might have done for him. When I refused to identify someone I didn't know, they transferred me to a camp at the Kozia station, near Donosha, on the Vorkuta-Kotlas route, where there were masses of Lithuanian, Estonian, and Latvian political prisoners.

"My life had ended. I was living on my memories; I was nineteen, and I felt like an old woman with nothing in front of me. Then I realized that a person is young as long as he makes plans for the future and the future is a mystery that attracts him, but at the same time frightens him. When this no longer happens, then he becomes old.

"After that I was taken to another camp. I was placed in the brigade of a man called Vasiliev. He was a military man who had participated in the war. Vasiliev sent Rita Panfilova, a fellow prisoner, and me to cut down trees. Of course, Rita and I had absolutely no experience, so we spent a whole day cutting down one tree. It was a tall pine. First we cut with a manual saw. The work was extremely slow, and on top of that I hated cutting down the body of a living thing. I felt more pain for the tree than if I were cutting myself. Finally, I pretended to saw, but I really was just trying to keep from hurting the pine. So, the only one working was Rita. After a while, the pine started to fall little by little, but it wasn't clear just which way it was falling. Rita and I were jumping around like goats to get away. When it finally reached the ground, we tried to drag it, but the branches got tangled in the other trees, and it was hopeless. We realized that we should have cut the branches, but it was too late. The foreman of the brigade was furious because we hadn't reached our quota. We made fun of him behind his back. Covered with the sticky pine resin, which gave off a fresh perfume, we smelled each other like dogs. We never got tired of the pure, calming scent of the woods.

"The next day, to punish us, we got only half a portion of bread and went without supper. That day they assigned me the task of gathering big branches of pine and burning them in a bonfire. I threw the branches onto the fire and, while they burned, I sat down close by to watch. Later, a man sucked in the air, sniffed like a dog, and then shouted: 'Something's burning!' I hadn't realized until then that some burning needles from the pine had fallen on my quilted pants. First a little spot burned, but in a fraction of a second all my clothes went up in flames. Everyone fell on me to help put out the fire. From then on, I had only burned rags to wear. On the way to work and at work too, I was colder than ever. Every day I came back from work frozen, hungry, and exhausted.

"It was intolerable. I refused to keep working. They put me in a solitary cell and gave me almost nothing to eat. I was cold day and night. And sleepless, since there was no bed. When I went back to the barracks three days later, the foreman, Vasiliev, refused to accept me. They sent me to cut posts; for fourteen hours a day, I had to work like a robot. How could I stand it? I often thought about the old shaman's words. He had advised me to search for something beautiful even when

I was exhausted. But I was so worn out that I didn't have the energy or the desire to do it, and so I didn't.

"I often refused to go to work. Each time I refused, they sent me into solitary, where there was no food and the cold kept me from sleeping. I became a *dokhodiaga*, a half-dead nag, which in Gulag slang is the term for prisoners that are near death. I accepted the idea that I was going to die. It was better than living like a slave."

{4}

Summer came. There was light day and night. In the early hours of the morning, the sky took on a deeper violet tone, but it quickly gave way to the sun, which pulled away from the horizon and stayed up for about twenty hours. Nobody could tell the difference between day and night. We couldn't sleep, and we collapsed from fatigue like flies at the end of the summer. Every day I dreamed about those huge mosquitoes. They don't bite as much as the little ones, but they're repulsive. At night, they seemed like hairy angels flying around my head. At least the nights were a little quieter; the bugs didn't bother us as much.

"They sent me to a different camp to do different work with different people. Part of our punishment was to make us lose our points of reference. As soon as we established a routine and got to know people, they would send us off to another camp with new people who had different ways to get on your nerves and different customs. There was no choice but to take it calmly, which in those difficult circumstances required a superhuman effort.

"They assigned me to the brickworks. Next to me, a tall, handsome blond man was working. He was obviously older than I. I was introduced to him, and he kissed my hand as if we weren't two filthy, flea-bitten, starving, half-asleep scraps of garbage dressed in rags who, for fourteen hours a day, hammered bricks in, one after another, but relaxed, perfumed people who had met each other at a reception, one in a cocktail dress with a glass of champagne in her hand and the other in a dark suit with a gray tie.

"'Heino Eller.'

"'Valentina Grigorievna Iyevleva. I'm pleased to meet you. You have the same name as a famous Estonian composer.'

"'That's who I am,' he answered, and I think he blushed.

"'When I was a student, we played your compositions.' I felt as though I had run into someone I knew from my former life. I felt like hugging him.

"'Anatoly Vaneev,' the prisoner who was working alongside Heino joined our conversation.

"The three of us went to the canteen together, and we soon became inseparable. Once I recited to them a few of the poems I composed before going to sleep and on the long walk to work to keep my mind busy. Heino Eller offered to compose music to accompany them. Later we presented them at our Saturday recitals."

"You had recitals?" I wonder.

"Yes," replies Valentina, slightly annoyed. "Very few camps had them. That camp organized recitals as a way to commemorate the Communist holidays and it became a weekly routine. So I convinced Anatoly to recite Gavrila Derzhavin. Standing in front of the public, with his shirt unbuttoned, he thundered in his deep bass voice:

I am a king, I am a slave,
I am a worm, I am God.

"And we all understood that he really was a king and he was God even though the authorities were doing everything in their power to turn him into a worm and a slave. We suddenly realized that all of us were kings and gods, no matter how much the camp tried to reduce us to worms and to make us carry out exhausting work fit for slaves in chains. We applauded the poet, Derzhavin, and the interpreter, Anatoly. But more than anything, we applauded ourselves, as a group and as individuals."

{5}

Valentina drinks a little more tea. Then she looks at her hands as though she doesn't recognize them. She smiles and says, "In that camp I met Tatiana, one of my great friends from the Gulag. An actress."

The old woman rolls her wheelchair to a shelf with a few books on it. She pulls out one of them. On the cover is a portrait of a woman whose smile makes her wide face even wider. Her face is framed by a Marlene Dietrich–style hairdo.

Valentina explains that it's an autobiography of Tatiana, the celebrated actor.

"I have to tell you her story; it's much more interesting than mine."

I don't want to interrupt her, so I just nod my head.

"I met Tatiana through Heino. She was thirty-five and famous. She was new to our camp, and she had nowhere to sleep, since all the pallets and bunks were taken. No one wanted to share a bed, so I gave her space, and at night she told me her story. We didn't want anyone to hear us, so—lying on the top bunk together, just under the ceiling—we whispered.

"At first sight, Tatiana's life was like a brilliant, deep red apple that anyone would want to take a bite of. Not many people realized that the apple was rotten inside. Tatiana Okunevskaya was enjoying extraordinary professional success in both the theater and film; she was our Greta Garbo. Artists and politicians admired her, and Marshal Tito of Yugoslavia asked her to marry him just before the war. I had seen her play the leading role in *Night Over Belgrade* and act with her company in the capital. However, Tatiana had two unfortunate marriages. Her second husband, Boris Gorbatov, was a writer who had sold out to socialist realism, and his books were artistic failures. More than art, what interested him was high-level politics. An opportunist, he became one of the directors of the Union of Soviet Writers, a position reserved exclusively for shoddy writers who were faithful Stalinists. Gorbatov dragged his wife to every possible political reception. For her birthday and her saint's day, he wrote her love poems that he published in newspapers and magazines so that the entire Soviet Union believed he was deeply in love. Everyone was convinced of it, except Tatiana; she felt there was no real connection between them, and she wept over it at night.

"Boris gave her no support. He dragged her to the receptions hoping that some of her shine would rub off on him. When they arrested Tatiana and condemned her to the Gulag, he repudiated her, annulling the marriage. In ideological cases, divorce wasn't even necessary. In her former life, as she referred to it—that is, before she was arrested—Beria had lured her to dinner once with the promise of freeing her father and her grandmother, who had both been condemned to the Gulag in the Great Purge of 1937. Tatiana accepted, because she didn't really have a choice. Beria took her to his dacha in the outskirts of the city, where he raped her. Of course, he didn't even bother to tell her that her grandmother and her father had died a long time ago, shot shortly after they'd been arrested. Tatiana only found out about that later."

{6}

O ne night my new friend woke me up. This was very strange, because it was still a long time before reveille," Valentina continued. "In a whisper so low I could barely make out the words, she told me that she had had a great love, an Indian. His aunt, Mrs. Vijaya Lakshmi Pandit, the sister of Prime Minister Nehru, was the ambassador of India to the USSR, and her nephew Triloki (whom Tatiana called Tikki, as did his friends) was helping her as an attaché to start up the first

Indian embassy in the Soviet Union. Tikki had studied in Oxford, just like his aunt.

"I am sure that they arrested and condemned Tatiana because of her relationship with Tikki. The same thing happened to me. In Stalin's time, relationships with foreigners were forbidden. That was reason enough for us Russians to like the idea. Tatiana and Tikki (his full name was Triloki Nath Kaul) met at a reception in the Indian embassy. Mrs. Pandit was easygoing, and the gathering was fairly informal. Tatiana's gaze met the brown, kohl-lined eyes of the young attaché more than once. Tikki reminded her of one of the gods in the Hindu pantheon: Krishna. The only thing missing was the flute. During the reception, he took her dishes of Indian specialties and explained the cultural context of each one. Afterward, he suggested that they go out together so that she could show him her favorite parts of Moscow, but it seemed that someone was following their car, so from then on, they always drove out of the city. They drove through the snowy countryside. When the snow had begun to melt, Tatiana spotted a white bellflower beside the road. Tikki stepped into the mud with his shiny shoes to pick the first flower of spring for her. He was a quiet man, who seldom got upset, but Tatiana saw tears in his eyes if she ever came late to their dates. He didn't know Russian, and Tatiana didn't speak English, but they understood each other.

"One day Tikki brought a document with him, because he wanted to show Tatiana something important. She managed to understand that they were watching him and following him. She understood that her friend was acting honorably to warn her even though it might mean the end of their relationship.

Tatiana didn't pay much attention to the warning: she was brave and a little reckless. She convinced herself she was a free woman who hadn't become a coward like her husband. More than that, taking risks made her feel her life was full. She didn't put an end to her dates with Tikki, but they began to see each other at his house.

"When his work as a diplomat ended in Moscow and he had to go back to India, Tikki gave her a sumptuous shawl of Indian silk. In the labor camp, Tatiana took care of it like a treasure. It was impossible to keep anything in the camps, but Tatiana managed to hold on to the shawl, because it meant so much to her.

"Later they arrested Tatiana, and from that point on, she could not maintain her correspondence with Tikki. He left Moscow. Back in India, he got married to a bride his parents had chosen, according to Hindu tradition, and had a daughter named Preeti. In the sixties, he became the Indian ambassador to the USSR, and—just imagine—he was named the godfather of Svetlana Alliluyeva, the daughter of Stalin, whose husband was an Indian. I say 'husband' even though our bureaucratic officials did not allow them to marry. He was named Brajesh Singh. He was a thorn in the side of Soviet power, and they hounded him to death.

"I think about Svetlana: she scattered Brajesh Singh's ashes on the Ganges, and from India she fled to the United States. This was in 1967. She didn't want to return to the Soviet Union, although she had to leave two teenage kids behind. After that she lived in the US and in England, never quite content, always looking for something more fulfilling; she even spent a few years at the Arizona outpost of the Taliesin Fellowship, a sort of sect led by Frank Lloyd Wright's Serbian widow, Olgivanna. Before Svetlana left them, married for the third time and with a baby girl, they had taken away all her money (she had earned millions of dollars with the sales of her books) in order to pay her husband's debts."

Valentina finishes the story: "Tikki kept the manuscript of Svetlana's first book, *Twenty Letters to a Friend*. It was published a little later in the US and became a worldwide success. That's the story of Tikki."

"How did you find all of that out?" I ask, incredulous.

"Through Tatiana, of course. During Tikki's second diplomatic mission to Moscow, they ran into each other a number of times at receptions. That was about ten years after she had returned from the camps. When she left the parties, he always watched her go with sad eyes. His marriage wasn't happy. His wife was a traditional Hindu, and she never traveled with him. Tikki spent more time with his daughter, a cosmopolitan young woman, than with his wife."

{7}

In 1948 Tatiana returned to Moscow from Kishinev, the capital of what was then Moldavia. Her theater company had been invited to perform there, and that time Boris, her husband, accompanied her. As an important Party official, he must have known that the secret service was supposed to arrest his wife soon, and he was worried about her. He wanted to be by her side. Even though he was a big shot in the Party, he could do nothing for her, because someone must certainly have told on Tatiana and there was no way around denunciations: the regime was based on them; they were sacred. Maybe someone wished her ill. Maybe it was done out of envy. Tatiana told me that only one close friend knew about her relationship with Tikki.

"Tatiana came back from Kishinev with the flu. Her husband insisted that she shouldn't fly, and the long train trip, even though it was by sleeping car, was hard on her. On the fifth day, when they came to arrest her, she had a fever of over a hundred and two degrees. Shaking with chills, she put on an elegant dress as if she were going to give a recital. She thought it was a misunderstanding that would be straightened out soon. All of us thought the same thing when our turns came, because we weren't conscious of having broken any rule.

"Viktor Abakumov, the minister of state security, was one of the people who interrogated her. He was interested in her relationship with foreigners, with the Yugoslav president, Marshal Tito, with Tikki, and with others. During one of those interminable late-night interrogations, he let them serve her coffee and cookies, which she, of course, didn't even taste. They made her repeat over and over how, at a reception, Tito had asked her for the first waltz. Compared to Beria, Abakumov was fairly decent. The other agents were rough and insisted that she admit her guilt right off. And, since it seemed that the whole business was going to go on for a long time, because Tatiana refused to confess and Lubyanka Prison was full to bursting, they locked her in the refrigerated room for hours so that her hands and feet would freeze. But she didn't confess even then. She fell sick again. The fever returned, and one day, in a state of complete exhaustion, she signed a confession saying she had acted as a spy passing secret information to foreign powers, all of it untrue. She was completely worn out by her imprisonment and the tortures she, like all of us, had suffered. There were physical tortures, since at night she was summoned regularly to interrogations and during the day she was not allowed to lie down or even to sit with her eyes closed (when that happened the cell doors opened immediately and the guard yelled that it was forbidden to sleep after reveille). But there were also psychological tortures, since the interrogators were rough with her and most of the time they only called her a 'whore,' or a 'slut' or a 'prozzy.'"

{8}

One night, she was sleeping restlessly. She beat her fists in the air and cried out things I couldn't understand. Finally, I realized what she was shouting: 'He's a vampire, just sucking the blood from the nation! Kill me! I can't take any more!'

"I shook her to wake her up. It was a disaster. What if one of the other prisoners understood what she was saying in her sleep and decided to tell on her to improve her own situation or to get back at her for something? They would try her again, and she'd probably get ten more years or even twenty-five.

"I finally managed to wake her up. She murmured as if overwhelmed by fever. 'My soul is rebelling. They can torture me, they can destroy my body, but not my soul. My soul is alive, and it's rebelling. Stalin is a vampire who damages, destroys, devastates us. Hitler tried to exterminate the Jews, the Communists, the Romani, but Stalin wants to annihilate the intelligentsia, the spirit of the nation. My father and my grandmother were lucky to be shot in 1939. I'm grateful that they weren't tortured year after year in the camps, that they didn't have to see this devastation of the spirit, this eternal, arbitrary humiliation.'

"A little later, reveille sounded. Tatiana was in a terrible state all that day. The next night, I told her not to say anything, not to get worked up, but she needed to get it all out. 'You know, Valya, in Lubyanka I thought that it was a plot to destroy what makes each of us an individual, but now I see that it doesn't just happen in prison and in the Gulag. The whole Communist system is determined to do the same thing: to annihilate people's individuality, to transform the whole nation into a flock of sheep. It's like a dystopian novel. And we don't realize what's going on. As long as they're not in prison, people think they're free, and yet they don't really have more rights than people who are in prison or in the camps. Maybe they sleep more and eat better, but as far as everything else goes, the government controls them, they follow them and listen to them outside like they do here; even in so-called freedom, people are denounced just as we were.'

"I gave Tatiana a sugar cube that I had put away in the rags I stuffed into my boots to make them fit. She began to calm down.

"At night she kept on with her stories. Once, she told me, when they were taking her back from an interrogation in prison, she thought she could hear the voice of her mother, who was in prison too. Her cry of 'Mamaaa,' resounded throughout the building, but there was no reply. Maybe it hadn't been her mother, or maybe it was and they wouldn't let her answer. The jailers put irons on Tatiana and took her to an underground cell that was very humid. She caught pneumonia there, and so they sent her to a work camp in Zhezkazgan, Kazakhstan.

"She was so sick and her fever so high that she could barely remember the trip. She knew that they had carried her on a litter, but she was in such a state with the fever that she only wanted to die."

{9}

One night she realized that she was lying on her back and that enormous stars were sparkling overhead. She had the feeling that if she put her arm out she could catch one. The snow was shining around her, and it was icing over beautifully. There was not a soul anywhere she could see, but in her bed, next to her, someone was lying down breathing in her face: 'Thank God you've come back to your senses. I'm your doctor, and a prisoner too. I'm Georgy Markovich Kaufman. Don't turn your face away; don't move. This is the only way you'll get well.'

"Doctor Kaufman breathed in her face like the animals in Bethlehem that warmed baby Jesus with their breaths. He looked in her eyes and calmed her with his gaze. He was so kind that Tatiana started to cry.

"She was lying in a folding bed set up in a street in the camp, between the barracks. The doctor explained that the infirmary was full of dying people. 'As soon as there's room, we'll move you in there, but it's not much warmer than here. It's so cold inside that everything freezes on us, just like here.' Tatiana was so moved by the doctor's compassion that tears poured down her face. He dried them with the palm of his hand.

"'You mustn't cry. Tears freeze right away. And no matter what, do not breath through your mouth. That would finish you off. Don't move. If you do the rags people from the barracks have brought to cover you up will fall off.'

"The doctor got up from the bed, and Tatiana saw a short, bent, gray-haired old man, who must have been over eighty. He turned back to her.

"'I have to go to the infirmary now to see the dying. Someone else will lie beside you and warm up your face. We're taking turns. You have a pulmonary abscess. We don't have anything to eliminate the pus. We don't really have any medicine. Your body will have to take care of itself on its own. You'll need all your strength for that. A lady has brought you some hot water.'

"Tatiana made a feeble attempt to smile, but the doctor reacted, 'Be careful! I'm telling you again: if the sickness takes hold of your lungs, there's nothing we can do for you. If people talk to you, don't try to answer.'

"Tatiana felt as though that old man was Jesus Christ, that he really didn't exist, but was an apparition in her dreams, a product of her fever. Later she found out that when he was a child after the Revolution, his parents had taken him to France, and that when he was grown, he had moved to Shanghai, where he opened a clinic that made a name for itself throughout China. At eighty-two he decided to spend what was left of his life in Russia, where he was accused of espionage and sentenced to twenty-five years in the Gulag.

"Tatiana got better little by little. In spring, a warm wind blew across the blanket of flowers that covered the desert of Kazakhstan. But soon the long Kazakh summer set in. A harsh sun fell on the hard, dry earth that the inmates—including a recuperated Tatiana—had to dig up and load with their shovels onto trucks. At night, Tatiana often collapsed on her bed from fatigue and fell asleep immediately without eating supper, without even the energy to undress."

{10}

Once Tatiana took off from work running, out of breath. Doctor Kaufman had sent a nurse to ask her to come immediately. He'd never done anything like that. 'I hope that nothing has happened to him,' she thought, speeding up. She found him standing at the door with a smile on his face. 'Come in. There's tea on the table and even a piece of white bread. Help yourself.'

"Tatiana gobbled it up, and the doctor got to the point: 'They've told me you refused to shake hands with the woman who runs the camp.'

"'I couldn't do it. Something in me refused to do it.'

"'Why take things to extremes?'

"'But she's a revolting warden!'

"'She's an inmate, just like you. You know perfectly well that in the camps the guards are also prisoners. On top of that, she got you a chicken to help you get stronger. She was sorry for you because she'd seen you in films. Even though it smelled bad, it was still a chicken! Not everybody would have done that for you. Don't you see that your pride is out of place here?'

"Tatiana remembered that she'd made broth with the chicken. She and her barracks mate Zhanna had had to pull the worms out of it, but the result was delicious! 'You're right,' she murmured. She felt she had to confess something to the doctor: 'You're going to get mad at me, even madder if that's possible, but I was so fed up that in a moment of desperation I wrote a letter to Stalin. I've already sent it. I was like somebody drowning who grabs a thread to hold on to.'

"'Good God! What did you write him?'

"'I told him everything that happens here.'

"'And do you really think the letter will reach him? In this country, letters don't usually reach the people they're addressed to. Instead, they fall into the hands of the people the authors of the letters are complaining about.'

"'I don't know. I hope my husband manages to give it to him.'

"'Even if the camp censors let it go, do you really believe it will change anything?'

"'Well . . . when Stalin realizes what's happening, then . . .'

"'Do you really think Stalin doesn't know about all this?'

"Tatiana stammered something. She realized what a risk she had run for no good reason. What would happen? What would become of her?

"The doctor continued, 'Stalin? He's not worried about our brilliant future; it's all a façade. Everything you see around you is his work. That marvelous future is a lie just like everything else Stalin has ever said or done. Stalin is dark, astute, a hypocrite, a coward. He's as ordinary and hardhearted and mean as all the other little men that have been raised up by the wave of history. What exactly did you write?'

"'I wasn't emotional. I described exactly what I had seen first in the prisons in Moscow—Lubyanka and Lefortovo— and then explained what I've lived through here in the camp.'

"'Do you realize what a huge risk you took?'

"'I can imagine.'

"At that point, Zhanna came running. Tatiana's shovel had gone missing, so they had condemned her to ten days in an isolation cell. People said you couldn't breathe the air in there. Everybody was afraid of it. But Tatiana told herself that it couldn't be worse than the refrigerator in Moscow, so she accepted calmly. She spent days and nights sitting on a stool, picking off the fleas that fell from the ceiling and jumped off the walls. Finally, they reduced the ten days to four, but she had to go straight to work just like the other women. They were constructing a canal. In a heat that reached 104 degrees, they had to lift up and roll fifty-kilogram stones and use their shovels to dig up and load the earth onto trucks. The earth was roasted; the nights were too short to cool the air. The women worked with grinding and pressing machines that gave off heat. Every rag they wore was soaked in sweat. Tatiana tried to imagine how Greta Garbo or Marlene Dietrich would withstand it.

"Suddenly her thoughts were interrupted: 'Tatiana Oku-nevskaya, go to the administration office!'

"'Her vision clouded over. That kind of order wasn't normal. It only happened in exceptional cases. She made herself keep calm. An order like that could mean death or freedom. The man in charge, a severe, unpleasant blond, started to interrogate her slowly and carefully, 'Had she written someone a letter? What contacts did she have? Who were her friends when she was free?' He was a shrewd interrogator. He didn't treat her like a prisoner, but like a person. Tatiana, well aware that the man was a chameleon, took great care not to get caught in his web.

"'Get ready for a trip. An order has come for you to present yourself in Moscow.'

"Could that really mean freedom? If I could just go home.... Home! What I would give to spend even a single night at home! She said good-bye to the doctor. It was the first time since they met that he looked happy even though his eyes showed a hint of fear that he was trying to hide.

"Tatiana sat on the bed of a truck with an armed soldier, who kept an eye on her so she wouldn't try to escape. As they drew away, Tatiana went from looking in the doctor's eyes to following his gray hair until his figure was lost in the distance. Then she looked at the camp and imagined the doctor there, until the camp too was reduced to a dot and then a cloud of dust in the distance. She realized that she would not see the doctor again, but, despite his age, she never dreamed that he would die just a few weeks after she left."

{11}

Tatiana once again found herself facing the doors of Lubyanka Prison. They took her through long passageways. A sepulchral silence pervaded the jail. They shut her in a cell on her own and left her there for whole weeks as if they'd forgotten about her. She began to lose her hope of being released. At last, one day a key clicked in the lock.

"'Time for an interrogation!'

"They led her to Abakumov's office. She knew him, but now the minister of state security didn't even look at her.

"'So . . . you're back here in Lubyanka. How does that feel?' It was the first time he had spoken to her in that way. Normally he joked; sometimes he almost flirted; in short, he acted like a man in the presence of a woman, but now he was cold and out of humor.

"'Why aren't you saying anything? You were better off in the camp, right? There a person can arrange things to suit herself, skip work, rest up in the infirmary, get packages of food from relatives, write letters.' He jumped at her in a fury: 'You must be an idiot! Do you know where your letter wound up? Here! It's in my desk! You thought you were smarter than this civil servant, right? You've become a real pig!' He shouted at her until he lost his voice. 'We'll see now who has the last word. According to you, I'm an enemy of the people, right? I am beating the Russian public to death! The Russian intelligentsia! To tell the truth, with scum like you there's nothing to do but kill you. According to you, I'm a murderer! I . . .'

"He raised his arm to strike her but stopped himself half-way. 'I won't dirty my hands with you. I'll let you rot in one of our underground cells where you've already had the pleasure of staying. I'll let you rot, let you freeze! I'll torture you until you die, understand? The problem is that with that brain the size of a mosquito you don't understand anything at all. Now, tell me, who was going to pass on your letter?

"'No one. I put it in the mailbox.'

"'So, you refuse to tell me. Fine, fine, I'll let you wait. I'll have your mother tortured, and then you'll see how glad you are to tell the truth!'

"'I don't know what else I can tell you.'

"'I'll put your mother in custody right now. And your hus-band, Gorbatov, that incurable womanizer, will keep on en-joying his wine and caviar, without lifting a finger for you. No one will lift a finger for you! Because nobody will know where you are.'

"He pushed a button: 'Take her away.'

"Tatiana crossed the room. In the door, she turned: 'I am absolutely certain of one thing: one day our positions will be reversed.'

"'Calm down,' she told herself, 'Don't say another word. If you do, he'll have another fit, and it will be worse for you. Calm down. Don't take any more risks!'"

{12}

For a year, the minister of state security left Tatiana in the cold, humid underground cell of Lubyanka, the most feared prison of all. For a year, she didn't hear any human voice except for the guards giving orders, and that was her only contact with a living soul. For a year, she shivered constantly from the cold and the rheumatism that consumed her wrists and knees. For a year, she ordered herself: 'You can't lose your mind; you can't give him that pleasure. And to keep sane, you have to establish a daily routine and stick to it.'

"She knew when it was day or night according to the time they brought her a watery soup. Every day she made herself walk four steps out and four steps back, from one wall of the cell to another, for half an hour in the morning and again at night. After her 'walk,' she exercised, and finally she put her brain to work: she recalled half-forgotten verses and little by little she forced them to emerge from the depths of her memory and she murmured them. Later she practiced them in a low voice, and when she was sure that she had the whole poem in her power, she recited it to herself. Every time she found new meanings. In the same way, she searched her memory for the roles she had played. Roxane in *Cyrano*, Ophelia in *Hamlet*, Masha in *The Three Sisters*. She thought about the characters and the works. If she had had a paper and pencil, she would have written entire essays about them.

"For a year she meditated too about the worst part of Soviet power. Its arbitrary nature, she decided. Yes, its arbitrary nature was the worst thing about it. If the minister of state security felt like it, he could put her in a cell that was covered with mold in the bottom of a prison where the sun didn't shine and no one ever came, and leave her there to rot as if it were a medieval dungeon, and he could do it with total impunity. 'Our whole system is founded on caprice,' she would whisper. For a year, depressing ideas and actual depression assailed her. Whenever she felt she would lose her mind out of desperation, she would get up and walk four steps out and four steps back. By walking, she kept her sanity and stayed to some extent in shape physically. She remembered close and distant friends, relatives, her family. She loved all of them, and she told herself that she'd be a better person than she was before if she survived the torture that was like something out of Dante's *Inferno*.

"One day, she decided to try to clean a little spot on the filthy window that looked out onto the dark passageway. Nothing ever happened. There was nothing to see. At least until one day when she saw Abakumov go by, followed by one of the guards with a machine gun aimed at his back. It seemed impossible. She thought it must be a hallucination brought on by the constant solitude to which she had been condemned.

"However, the next day they came for her. They had to carry her in their arms because she had become so weak. She suddenly found herself in a hospital cell. At first, her stomach could not tolerate the food intended for sick people. At night, she couldn't sleep. She couldn't shake the notion that they would shoot her soon, as they had done to her father and her grandmother. She didn't want to accept the sleeping pills offered by the nurse for fear they were trying to poison her.

"After a week of treatment, they called her for an interrogation. Two men held her under her arms and dragged her to the office. After spending a year in the tiny cell, she was in such poor shape that she could hardly stand up. Besides, she had lost the habit of speaking and, in the interrogation, she wasn't able to say a word. She could only make sounds like an animal. Her exercise routine in the tiny space of her cell sufficed to keep her alive, but she must have lost the power of her muscles; similarly, her personal recitals couldn't keep her voice strong enough. A new, gentler interrogator sent her back to the hospital cell and recommended that she write down everything she remembered. He especially wanted to know anything related to Abakumov. Tatiana gave him a questioning look. Abakumov? What was that about? In a kindly way she had not experienced for years, the interrogator told her that Abakumov had fallen from favor. They had arrested him, and now he was a prisoner in Lubyanka just like she was. That's why they had to review the cases that had passed through his hands.

"After another week of care, they called her for another interrogation. By that time, she could walk and talk. In addition to the interrogator from the last time, an older man in a general's uniform was present.

"'Good morning. I'm the inspector general for the Military of the Soviet Union, and I need to ask you a few questions. Did you have a relationship with Abakumov? Did you go to bed with him?'

"'No.'

"'Did you make him any proposition of that sort?'

"'No.'

"'Did you write any illegal letters from the labor camp?'

"'No.'

"'Before they took you to the labor camp, who interrogated you here in Lubyanka?'

"'Abakumov.'

"'What did he ask you?'

"'He asked me about a reception given by the president of Yugoslavia, Tito.'

"Tatiana remembered that in the last interrogation before they took her to the work camp in Zhezkazgan, Abakumov had asked her repeatedly about her waltz with Tito. She didn't give many details in her answers, saying she didn't remember even though she remembered every single detail. During the waltz, Tito had suggested that she move to Yugoslavia, work there, and become his wife. In the same light tone he had used, she rejected his proposition (laughing, she said that a person has only one home), but she thought often about that proposition and the waltz and her earlier encounters with Tito.

"She had given Abakumov short answers, primarily because she didn't want to let him in on her private life, but also because she had the feeling that someone else was hiding in the room, behind the stove or in the next room behind a door. During these interrogations, Abakumov kept looking toward the door, and that made her suspicious.

"'What did Abakumov want to know about Tito's reception?'

"'What dress I was wearing.'

"'What else?'

"'What the marshal and I had talked about during the waltz.'

"'And what did you tell him?'

"'That I didn't remember.'

"'Is this your writing?' They gave her a crumpled piece of her letter to Stalin.

"'Yes.'

"'Tell us what you talked about in this letter.'

"'About everything I saw and heard around me. About my experience.'

"'Who was the letter written to?'

"'To my husband, Gorbatov. He was supposed to hand it over to Stalin, since he gets together with him often in his work.'

"'How did it get to Abakumov's table?'

"'I have no idea.'

"She imagined that when he fell out of favor, Abakumov had torn it up into little pieces. 'Why, for God's sake, didn't he throw it into the stove since he had a big one in his office?' she asked herself, and she answered her own question, 'Because he didn't have time.' When someone falls out of favor, he has very little time to destroy everything that might lead to an accusation against him.

"'Now, go back to your cell and, taking your time, describe for us everything related to Abakumov. I believe you when you say there was nothing between you, but I think you must have known each other before.'

"He was right. She could picture Abakumov at a reception, hidden behind a column and following her with his eyes. She had warned her husband, who said the minister had nothing to do at a reception for artists and that he couldn't understand why the man was there.

"They transferred Tatiana to a common cell with other inmates. She wrote what they asked for. A little later, they sent her to another work camp. Her case had been reviewed; she had been exonerated, and they were about to free her, but in the meantime Minister of State Security Abakumov was rehabilitated. Only Stalin or Beria, first deputy chairman of the Council of Ministers, could have ordered his rehabilitation. So they sent Tatiana to a camp that was harsher than the Kazakh camp in the Karaganda region; they sent her to a camp beyond the Arctic Circle."

{13}

And that's the story of Tatiana. In one of those camps up in the north I met her," says Valentina, getting more comfortable in her wheelchair. "They freed her in 1954, after Stalin died. Her husband died that same year, and another person as well: Abakumov. Tatiana had read the future correctly: there was a reversal of roles. But she didn't foresee, she couldn't foresee, that after Stalin's death, they would try Abakumov, condemn him for high treason, and shoot him at the end of that year."

After a moment of stunned silence, I ask Valentina exactly where she had met Tatiana.

"In Viatlag, near Vorkuta. I've already told you that I met her through Heino, the great composer, the prisoner who was a friend to both of us.

Valentina sips her tea, which has become cold. She makes a disgusted face and gets ready to fix another. While she's doing it, she continues her story:

"It was wonderful that the camp directors asked Heino to put on two performances that would be appropriate for our camp but that we could also present in neighboring camps. The system of the Gulag archipelago was made up of more than two thousand prisoners and hundreds of guards, group leaders as well as the administration, which was itself made up of prisoners. One of the performances should be theatrical and the other musical, with a chorus. Heino would be the playwright, the theater director, and the director of the choir. He couldn't say no. If he did, they'd have transferred him to another, harder camp as punishment."

"Did you and Tatiana act in those performances?" I ask.

Valentina pours out the freshly made tea and keeps on talking, "Tatiana and I were given the lead roles in the play, and we also sang in the chorus of the musical. Since Heino needed more singers in the choir, he picked other prisoners. Some of them were being punished for robbery, prostitution, or homicide. They used tons of makeup when they came to the rehearsals; they cursed nonstop and used filthy language in general. During the dance that was part of the musical, they lifted their skirts up way too high. Heino set the tone. He didn't allow that kind of behavior in his presence, but his influence was due primarily to his personality and character. The truth is that after a few weeks, these hard women had started to change. I'd never have believed it possible. It's not just that they stopped being provocative, but that they began using less makeup and doing a better job with it, and their table manners improved. That's the influence that Heino had on all of us.

"One of the prostitutes, Liuba, at first used a very bright pink lipstick that covered not just her lips but her teeth and even her nose, and she covered herself with quantities of a liquid that smelled terrible and that she thought was perfume. The whole idea was to stay in Heino's company, because whoever acted in the play or sang in the chorus had a shorter work schedule. The work involved laying brick or cutting down trees, chopping up tree trunks and building railroad tracks. Tatiana belonged to the forest brigade. The trees in Siberia are hundreds of years old, tall, enormous. More than once someone had her neck or her backbone broken when a tree fell on top of her, so getting a reduced workload was worth the effort.

"Under the influence of Heino and Tatiana and others, Liuba began to use less makeup, to substitute dried herbs for perfume. She dropped the filthy talk and pulled back her mop of hair in a ponytail. Although she tied it with a shoelace, which was all she could find in the camp, she did it with so much flair that, against her corn-colored locks, it looked like a special accessory. Other women from the group of thieves and prostitutes underwent a similar transformation.

"Why is it so much harder for a performance to be successful in the outside world? Why is it that when people are free
they don't have that collective perception of theater and their
applause is much more moderate? This is what Tatiana and I
wondered. We repeated each piece three times. Afterward,
we put on two of the performances in neighboring camps.
Around Vorkuta, in the north of Russia, tons of people would
come, and the spaces were packed. We were hugely successful
everywhere. Tatiana was a big draw, of course. All the prisoners had seen her films, and her presence lent a special glow to
our performances."

{14}

It was on December 31. During work, Heino invited me to
a New Year's Eve party. I knew this meant that I'd have to
escape in secret from my barracks, which closed at ten. I told
Heino to count on me although I knew it would be difficult
to leave my barracks and sneak into the men's camp. This is
what I did: I made a big doll out of rags. I put it on my bed
and covered it with a blanket. Later I jumped over the fence
and ran to the entrance where Heino, Anatoly, and a few other
men were waiting for me. We slipped away down the streets
until we reached a barracks in the men's camp.

"There we were greeted by warmth and the chiaroscuro
of candles that Anatoly's parents had sent from Leningrad for
the occasion, not to mention a cake and strudel and an apple

pie with raisins and nuts. Heino had been sent goose fat with cracklings, and we spread it on slices of bread that his room-mate, the camp's baker, had brought. To go with it, we had hot water seasoned with tea leaves and sugar. At midnight, we toasted the new year, and we hugged each other. I treated them to various American songs that Bill used to sing.

"Later someone knocked on the door. Silence fell over our room. Everybody froze in the position he was in at that mo-ment: Heino with the plate of bread and goose fat he was pass-ing around, Lena with an unlit match she was going to light a new candle with, Anatoly with his index finger in the air in the middle of a joke. We looked at each other almost stupefied. Then we heard louder knocks at the door.

"Anatoly recovered slowly and lowered his arm. He mo-tioned for me to hide and he went to open the door. I slid under the table as fast as I could. Anatoly put his coat on top of it, went out, and closed the door behind himself. Heino hid me behind an enormous barrel of yeast that Anatoly's room-mate had for his breadmaking. Lena hid behind there too.

"After a few minutes, Anatoly came back in with a guard. I sat on my haunches behind the barrel, as quiet as a mouse. I barely breathed, and I had to make an effort to keep my teeth from chattering, because away from the stove an icy wind blew through the cracks in the barracks. It must have been almost morning by then. From their conversation, I understood that someone had found a rag doll in my bed, and they were looking for me. Anatoly offered the new arrival a slice of bread with goose fat, and the guard accepted. Anatoly guaranteed that he hadn't seen me. The guard took his word and left."

{15}

They woke me up early in my barracks. The first thing I thought was: my mother says that what a person does on January 1 is what she'll do all year long. The guard shouted that I had left the barracks after ten at night, that she had found a sort of scarecrow in my bed, in my place, and that she was looking on it as an attempt to escape.

"'What attempt to escape? Didn't you find me sleeping peacefully in my bed?'

"But the guard wasn't listening to me. She yelled: 'Today we're transferring you! We're sending you on foot to another camp. You'll see how nice that is!'

"After the New Year's Eve get-together, I was still in a good mood, and I thought that if my mother's motto was true, all year long I would walk fifty kilometers on ice after an all-night party, heading to an unknown destination, probably an unwelcoming spot, far from the friendships I had formed in the last months."

Valentina pauses for a long time and looks through the window. The wind is blowing the snowflakes, which are denser and denser. I realize that she has no desire to keep on. She's tired, and surely what's coming is hard to deal with. I smile, trying to encourage her to continue. With distaste, Valentina drinks a little and dips a cookie in the tea before eating it.

"In the new camp it was almost all women," she says with a certain lack of interest, in a low voice. "Many were pregnant; they had come from different camps. The first thing I experienced was how cold it was in the barracks. During the day, we went to the forest to work as woodcutters, even the pregnant women. With every step we sank into the snow over our knees, halfway up our thighs, often up to our waists or higher. With every step, we had to rescue each other from the snow. In the morning, instead of the pathetic four hundred grams of bread they routinely doled out to us, we were given two hundred. There was no soup, but water that had been warmed up again. It was a world of pain and suffering, and yet all around us was the overwhelming beauty of the forest!"

{16}

It was the end of autumn. First, we received an order to dig a hole in the ice of the Ob River. Later, they carried us across the frozen river and left us on terra firma. Ice, snow, and dark: that would be our destiny for months, we knew.

"'We've arrived,' the conductor said.

"But we didn't see barracks, baths, or a camp of any sort.

"'Each of you will have to make your own spot as best you can,' he said.

"It turned out that the transport vehicle had brought about ten small tents that were not remotely enough for all of us. I was lucky: I was invited to share one of them with a lot of other women. We knew that the ones who didn't have a tent would freeze to death.

"In the morning, they divided picks and shovels between us.

"'Start digging!'

"The earth was covered with a hard blanket of frozen snow. It was impossible to dig through it. The picks simply bounced off the white surface, emitting a metallic sound. All day long, I pretended to dig; if not, the guards would have hit me with the butts of their rifles as they did with the other women.

"We hadn't bathed for a month. Soon the lice—big and white—showed up. I had never seen them like that. We crushed them on the stove. They hid in the seams of our clothes. As soon as we flattened one, two more appeared in the same spot. They bit us while we worked, and they didn't let us sleep.

"I protested to the directors. As a punishment, they reduced my portion of bread by half. I refused to go to work, and they assigned me an even harder job: laying the railroad tracks."

{17}

We walked in the dark to the place we were going to work. On our way, we told each other stories from our lives and made-up tales so the time would pass faster and so everybody who listened would think about something besides the trained dogs that herded us. I remembered the story about the queen of the ice and her evil kingdom. Living there had such an ill effect on little Gerd in the tale that he too became evil. Would we become like little Gerd? All the women around me sighed.

Once upon a time, there was a hunter named Poy-yaumbe, who was chasing a bear. The bear hid in a hole, and Poy-yaumbe went in search of him. The bear went farther and farther into the cave until Poy-yaumbe reached the end and found himself in a land like ours: there were forests, meadows, and villages, but everything was prettier. The sun shone brighter, and the people looked happy. There were grapevines growing and mulberries, lemon trees, and banana trees. But Poy-yaumbe paid no attention to all that beauty, because he wanted to go home. That night he had a dream. The spirit of the banana tree appeared and told him how to find his way. But once he had gotten home, Poy-yaumbe realized he missed that beautiful land. He was sad and felt he couldn't live without that sun and that happy countryside. In another dream, the spirit of the banana tree appeared again. This time it told him, "Poy-yaumbe, you will die soon, and then you'll live forever in that beautiful country. It's an underworld. A beautiful princess chose you as her husband. She became a bear in order to lure you to her world, but you were determined to return to your sad land. Now you'll have to make peace with the princess." Poy-yaumbe died soon after; he reached the underworld and lived happily with the beautiful princess forever after.

"So, girls, when we get to work and start digging, just tell yourselves that maybe we'll dig our way to a more beautiful world!

"I looked at the landscape spread out around our section. In the work camp, a person lost the custom of looking at the horizon, because life at the camp consumed us, just like the sea absorbs a grain of sand. I saw the usual panorama: under the dark gray sky, the icy white desert stretched out as far as I could see. I took hold of the pick and hit the ice with it. A chunk flew out, but the pick did not break through the frozen surface to the ground below. A guy named Sasha came up to watch my futile efforts. Then with his pick, he dug a portion of the road for the train track, and after helping me he disappeared like a ghost, just as if he had never been there.

"I don't know how many times I thought of taking off! But, how could I escape when every movement was watched by guards with shotguns? And where would I go, north of the Arctic Circle, where a person is surrounded by thousands of kilometers of tundra covered with snow and ice, a place buffeted day and night by snowstorms? The only thing we could do was try our hardest to survive, hold on to each moment of happiness that appeared as briefly as a butterfly and then flew off. We held on to those moments like a dog with a piece of meat. If we didn't, we'd die."

{18}

After another attempt at rebellion, I found myself in solitary confinement, it was just as cold inside the cell as it was outside. I was covered with bruises from the blows I'd been given, my backbone hurt, I was hungry and more dead than alive. I thought about my friend Nina, who had committed suicide. I decided to do the same. The idea was comforting. I was so desperate that I didn't see any other way out. Suddenly, I began to feel free, and that gave me strength.

"Two weeks later, when they had taken me out of solitary, I went to the work area. There were tubs filled with quicklime. I ran to them, found a big glass, and filled it with the stuff. Right away, I drank it down. I felt a terrible burning sensation as if my stomach had been scalded. My insides were in flames, and I wanted to throw up.

"They took me to the infirmary, but the nurse didn't know what to do with me. She gave me permission to skip work and installed me in a bed. For a few weeks, I was in pain, and the only thing I wanted was to die. During that whole time, I couldn't eat or drink. Not a single drop of water entered by stomach, everything came out immediately through my nose.

"A friend, blond Liosha, heard a few weeks later what had happened. He found food for me and paid for it himself: beef, sugar, and heavy cream. He brought me hot broth three times a day, then hot water with sugar and finally the cream. Little by little, my stomach accepted some of that food.

"Liosha sat down on my bed and said, 'You'll live, Valya. You have to live. You can only survive the camp if you have common sense, if you're intelligent, strong, skilled, astute, and a little devious.'

"Tortured, I shook my head. I didn't have the strength to think about being astute and a little devious. Liosha kept whispering, 'Don't you see that simple men and women are dying like flies all around you? Not to mention the old and the weak. Isn't that true, little one?'

"I agreed, especially because I wanted him to keep on talking. His sweet words whispered in my ear and his tenderness comforted me.

"'You can't say what you think. That's a defect, and it would be fatal for you. You have to keep on remembering that you're innocent, that you're here unjustly, that you haven't done anything to anybody. That conviction will help you. That's why so many murderers die here. It's because they know they're not pure and innocent.'

"Where had that guardian angel come from, that angel who sat down on my bed every day and fed me so patiently?"

{19}

One day Liosha didn't show up. Zina, a friend from my barracks, told me that they had sent him to another place without any warning, surely to keep him from taking care of me. I survived thanks to my angel Liosha, although my stomach was ruined for good.

"Was I happy to be alive? Not really. I didn't have any reason to keep on living. When I was well again and went back to work, even though my stomach wasn't really right, I decided to escape. I didn't care that it was almost impossible in winter, that a person couldn't get anywhere alone, that I would probably wind up frozen in the tundra. I wanted to get away even if that meant an almost certain death.

"On finishing my work, I put on all the clothes I had. I put my work pants and my overcoat on over my dresses. At night, prisoners who had permission left the camp with the guards to go to the store, where they could exchange coupons for food. I pretended to be part of the group and managed to get to the store. When I got there, I went to a dark corner where I knew there was a door, hoping that it wouldn't be locked. It was open! It seemed like a sign that I would get my wish. I was shaking with fear and an anguish that nearly paralyzed me. I went out and headed to the woods on the nearest icy path.

"There was no moon that night. The forest was dark, but the snow shone with its own light. With every step, my pants rustled. The sound made me think that they had found me, that they were on my heels. I had to skirt any place where I might run into a guard. In some spots, I sank into the snow up to my knees or my waist. I could have gone all the way under, as if it were quicksand, and there'd be nobody to rescue me. Other areas were frozen over, and I had no choice but to walk very carefully over the ice. At one point, I stumbled, and my pants made so much noise that they could probably be heard all over the woods. I heard a whooshing sound: the guards on skis. They were hot behind me! I turned around, but nobody was there. It was the sound of the woods, where snow and chunks of ice were constantly falling off the limbs of the trees. The sky was cloudy. It was surely going to snow. The moon was invisible, but the snow gave off such a gleam that I could see the woods as if it were day.

"I kept up a good pace all night, without getting tired. I was panicked, but my whole soul longed for freedom. After a long time, I began, slowly and weakly, to feel a kind of pleasure, and I started to sing in a low voice. When the dense darkness began to dissipate, I realized that morning was breaking and they would find me more easily. I sped up. I was walking on an unfamiliar path and didn't know where it would lead.

"'Barbed wire!' I shouted silently.

"And then I was set upon by guards who grabbed me violently and carried me somewhere. To a camp. Had I circled back to my own camp in the night? The guards led me to an office and then to a cell where I spent the rest of the night pacing. Two steps forward and two steps back. I was too afraid of what they might do to sleep.

"A little later, guards came from our camp to take me back. They put chains on me. Sometimes they spit on me or pushed me hard so that I kept falling down. At our camp, they led me to a room where four strong men began punching me. They were furious, because I had tricked them, because I had escaped so easily without their realizing it. I fainted, and when I came to, I was in the infirmary. My skin was swollen, and I was covered with bruises. My ribs were killing me; it was unbearable. They must have been fractured. They took me from the infirmary to the solitary cell with no time to heal.

"How long was I in solitary? Could it be ten days now? Or had they increased the sentence without telling me? I didn't know. I didn't know anything. And I wouldn't find out. I lived in darkness. It was at least ten days. When I looked outside through the crack between the beams, I saw the snow-covered tundra extending to the taiga: a white expanse bathed in moonlight as if some god from Olympus were holding an enormous lantern and illuminating the world."

{20}

Finally, I was liberated. I left the camp. Once I was in Arkhangelsk, I found out that my mother had died. My daughter Bella had spent ten years in an orphanage. When I went to get her, she didn't recognize me, and the teacher had to intervene to make her go with me.

"They forbid me to live in my city or, for that matter, in any other city. The former prisoners had to stay at least one hundred kilometers away from the capitals. In a vain effort to start living a normal life, I took Bella and went to visit the parents of my friends from the Gulag. I didn't have anybody else. We traveled a long way, to the southwest of the USSR, to different towns in Ukraine, and from there we went to Uzbekistan. From the southeast of the Soviet Union we took a route that led directly to the north, to Salekhard, a small city near the work camps. Nowhere could I find what I longed for: a peaceful life for Bella and me. The jobs they begrudgingly offered me did not last long. People were afraid to give a regular job to an ex-prisoner. I finally got an illegal job as a cleaner in an office.

"I got married later although I soon discovered that my husband had a taste for drink. I had more children, but what really made my life livable was reading. Gradually, my apartment filled up with hundreds, then thousands of books that began to take up almost all the space; they were the real inhabitants. I couldn't stop reading. It was my pastime, my passion, and my intellectual sustenance. Reading, I forgot about my wasted life, my complex identity, the reactions of people who treated me as if I had the plague. By reading, I could enjoy a new life, start over again, live many different lives."

{21}

The afternoon light has grown weak by the time Valentina finishes her story. We have nothing to say. Then, she breaks the silence and adds in a low, meditative voice: "I have known great goodness, great kindness, but also an evil that destroys everything. I experienced both things in the labor camps, and that has helped me understand other people and myself. All that has given me a profound knowledge of life. I've known people who saved my life by giving their own. And enemies who attacked me with a knife. More than once, I decided that it's possible to survive the Gulag, but not for most of the people in it. In liberty, everything is understated, easy, but you only learn to know yourself in extreme situations. In the camps, I learned to recognize evil: inflicting pain for no reason. Animals don't do this, only humans. But human beings can also do good deeds for no reason. And someone who has never experienced friendship in a concentration camp can't imagine what it is. It is something you can't find anywhere else."

I remember Tatiana.

"Did you see Tatiana after both of you were released?" I ask.

"I did. But she went back to acting and to her glamorous surroundings, so our worlds became so different that after a time I started avoiding her. I preferred the company of my books."

Later on I research Tatiana's life: before being sentenced to the Gulag, she was raped by Lavrentiy Beria, Stalin's deputy premier, at his dacha. She spent six years in the camps. Following her release from Steplag in 1954, she returned to the theater.

Valentina stops talking just as it grows dark outside and the lights go on in the apartment buildings across the street. With her bright eyes, she looks at the pink, turquoise, and yellow windows that light up in the darkness. And then she says: "Sometimes I think about my dead friends and family. I wonder what mattered most in their lives. The Gulag with its steadfast friendships? Did they have a guardian angel like Liosha? I wonder about all this, serenely, while I look at the colored windows. I imagine the life behind those windows, and in this way I come back to life. This is my hope, my daily drama, my happiness."

ANTIGONE FACING THE KREMLIN

Natalia Gorbanevskaya

{1}

On a gray day in Paris, in November 2012, a mass of people—mainly immigrants, most of them poor—is buzzing around the entrance to the Alesia metro stop. Natalia Gorbanevskaya lives nearby. I cross a small garden and continue down a passageway that leads to the apartment that is home to this famous journalist, dissident, and poet.

{2}

A strong, agile woman, who looks about seventy, opens the door. She greets me with a faint smile, but her gestures are nervous. In a low voice—which will become vigorous and even brusque when she talks about her experiences—she asks me to leave my coat on the bed, which is a mattress on the floor, covered with a pile of blankets. A picturesque disorder characterizes the one-room apartment. Everything suggests that Natalia Gorbanevskaya is not concerned about where she lives because she has more important things on her mind.

We sit at a little table spread with books and papers, overflowing ashtrays, plates and cups—a Meissen set—with what's left from breakfast. Natalia, who translates authors like Czesław Miłosz from Polish to Russian, and is one of the best-known dissidents of the Soviet regime, gets directly to the point. She uses one of the cigarettes she's never without like a firearm to warn the other person off any area that's too private. Her narration focuses on what happened in 1968. She speaks objectively, avoids sentimentality, and doesn't mince words.

{3}

On September 21, 1968, very early, as usual, I turned on the radio to listen to the Voice of America. In an almost frenzied tone, the newsreader was announcing that the night before the armed forces of the Warsaw Pact countries had invaded Czechoslovakia. I tuned in to other Western radio stations. All of them talked about the Soviet tanks that now occupied Prague. Then I listened to the Soviet station, Radio Mayak (the Beacon). They read the declaration from TASS, the Soviet news agency, with the same news. I didn't have to go to work that day, because I was on maternity leave, so I called my friend Larisa Bogoraz.

"'Lara, they've sent the army into Czechoslovakia.'

"What had happened was very serious. I didn't think an article in *A Chronicle of Current Events*, the dissident journal I directed, would be an adequate response. The invasion did not involve an internal Soviet matter, but an initiative our leaders had organized to punish what was, in fact, a sovereign country, even though it fell within our zone of influence.

"As a dissident, I had made a name for myself in the West. I had known Anna Akhmatova and had worked out the best way to smuggle *Requiem*, her great cycle of poems, into the West. And, by the way, it was thanks to her advice and her encouragement that I learned the art of poetry.

"After giving some thought to the issue, I decided that the only way to respond to the occupation of Czechoslovakia was a demonstration. When I found out from my dissident colleagues that plans were underway for a march, I decided to take part in it. I saw it as my duty. At that point I was nursing my newborn son, so I decided to carry the baby and a little Czech flag to the march.

"Larisa Bogoraz and I agreed: the demonstration would take place on August 25 at noon in Red Square in a spot that was once used for executions. The day before, Viktor Fainberg, another comrade, had arrived from Leningrad. He knew nothing about our plans in Moscow. Since the phones were bugged, we hadn't called him. He came to see me right away, and as soon as I opened the door, he said, 'We have to do the right thing and organize a protest. My friends in Leningrad say that I won't find anybody crazy enough to go to a march when they're almost certain to be arrested, but I've decided to do it, and I will even if I'm the only one.'

"I got him to calm down by telling him that he wouldn't be alone, that we'd organized a demonstration and that, yes, there were people in Moscow crazy enough to show up. By the way, talking about Viktor, they gave him a terrible sentence: he spent four years in the psychiatric hospital of a jail that hired former prisoners who had served time as robbers and murderers. They beat the inmates just for fun. I felt guilty for letting Viktor get involved in a protest that ended in that kind of torture, but if I hadn't told him about our protest, he would never have forgiven me.

"We let quite a few people know about it, all of them dissidents. Some of them didn't find out about the gathering, because their partners were afraid to tell them. Others showed up at Red Square, but didn't have the nerve to join the protest, because they figured they'd have to pay too high a price for their ideals."

{4}

On August 25 at noon, eight of us met on Red Square, on the site that, before the October Revolution, had been reserved for executions. I showed up with a baby buggy I'd borrowed. In it, I'd put my three-month-old son and our posters. We decided to gather on the sidewalk holding up our homemade posters. The posters said: 'Shame on the Invaders!' and 'Standing Up for Our Freedom and for Yours.' Mine was the only one with that last slogan. It meant: 'When you Czechs are free, then we Russians will be free too,' even though nobody entertained much hope of seeing freedom in our country. Another of my posters read 'Hands Off Czechoslovakia!'

"It was the fourth day after the occupation, and Soviet propaganda was at its peak. The regime asked Soviet citizens to provide their 'fraternal support to the Czech and Slovakian peoples, who have been led astray by all the lies propagated by the imperialistic powers of the West.'

"People who crossed the square concentrated on looking elsewhere. Later I found out that they were KGB agents dressed as civilians. They soon started to yell in their loudest voices, 'Filthy Jews!,' 'Traitors!' and 'Let's beat up the anti-Soviet scum!' The KGB agents tore up our posters and Czech flags. We kept quiet and remained sitting on the curb without offering any resistance.

"Later the beatings began. A man struck Litvinov with his briefcase, and a woman hit him with her purse. A man punched Fainberg until he lost four teeth. All that lasted six, seven, eight minutes, tops. Then the secret police took away the protesters. They didn't just take them away, they dragged them off and sent them directly to prison. They ignored me.

"While they were taking the protesters to prison in the police car, another car drove out of the Spassky Gate of the Kremlin. Among the passengers was Alexander Dubček, the deposed leader of the Prague Spring. The night of the invasion, the Soviets had flown him in handcuffs to Moscow.

"The KGB carried out its arrests very quickly so that Western eyes would not realize what had happened, and, in effect, the event initially went unnoticed in the West. However, the news about our demonstration and the subsequent arrests ultimately reached the Western media."

At this point I remember that the Czech-born British playwright Tom Stoppard wrote a play about the protesters' bravery on Red Square, and Joan Baez composed a song named "Natalia" about Gorbanevskaya and her activism. In her concerts and on her album *From Every Stage*, Baez precedes it with a little introduction in which she says: "It is because of people like Natalia Gorbanevskaya, I am convinced, that you and I are still alive and walking on the face of the earth."

> *Weaver of words*
> *Who lives alone*
> *In fear and sorrow*
> *Where are the words*
> *To set you free*
> *Perhaps tomorrow*
> *Where is the earth*
> *Where is the sky*
> *Where is the light*
> *You long for*
> *What hope of you*
> *Where you are now*
> *Natalia Gorbanevskaya*
>
> *Inside the ward*
> *Naked and cruel*
> *Where life is stolen*
> *From those who try*

To stay alive
And not be broken
Where are the friends
Where are the men
Who among them
Can defend you
Where is the child
You'll never see
Natalia Gorbanevskaya

What else there lives
Behind the door
That never opens
Are you insane
As they say you are
Or just forsaken
Are you still there
Do you still care
Or are you lost forever
I know this song
You'll never hear
Natalia Gorbanevskaya

Natalia Gorbanevskaya

Natalia goes on with her story:

"Those Western voices were crucial to us, because they gave us the feeling that there were people who heard us and supported us, that we weren't alone and that our protest, which

contested the Kremlin's right to intervene in the internal affairs of their satellite countries, made sense. That was essential
to us: knowing there was some meaning to the suffering that
followed our action almost immediately.

"It *was* worthwhile. In different Russian cities people heard
about our march. As a result of our public opposition, they
started to protest as well: they produced informative flyers
and stuck them on the walls of their cities at night.

"For me, it was particularly worthwhile, because if I hadn't
done it, I would never have forgiven myself."

{5}

After the others were arrested, I was the only one who
kept up the demonstration in Red Square until, a little
later, they came back and took me off for a series of interrogations. Afterwards, they went home with me and searched
my apartment. In the meantime, as I found out later, they had
imprisoned the other protesters. Thanks to having little children, but also to being the most famous dissident in the West,
they didn't arrest me at that point. They wouldn't do it until
a year later, in December 1969, declaring me mentally ill. According to a psychiatrist, I suffered from progressive schizo-
phrenia. It's how they usually diagnose objectors.

"They shut me up in the psychiatric hospital in the Butyrka
prison and subjected me to treatment. Then they transferred
me to the psychiatric prison in Kazan, a special center for 'enemies of the people.' The building was surrounded by a wall

topped with barbed wire, and the windows were barred—just like any other prison."

Natalia becomes quiet. She doesn't feel like saying any more. Then she explains her silence: "Being shut up in one of those psychiatric centers, which in colloquial Russian we call *psikhushka,* is the worst thing that can happen to a person. I've never spoken about it. I've never been able to speak about it. To tell the story would be like going through the torture all over again."

Her silence is eloquent.

She finally decides to talk about her experience even though the narration leaves her unsettled and anguished. She speaks hurriedly, as if wanting to get it over with as soon as possible.

{6}

They gave me psychotropic drugs that in the long term induce Parkinson's disease and also lead to memory loss. In the case of my roommate—she was also a political prisoner—her fingers began to tremble after a few months. She somehow managed to get books in secret, which she shared with me, but neither of us could remember anything. We'd read a page or a few lines and then forget what we had just read.

"There was no way to get rid of the medications. They watched the patients like hawks. I tried to hide my medicine a number of times, but they threatened me with the severest punishment. I felt as though I were chained to the bed. When it was time for our walk, I wanted to fly away and shake off my chains.

"Once a month, the prisoner patients were allowed to write a letter up to four pages long. As soon as I started writing, I'd forget what I had already written and what was left to be said. It was an exhausting experience. The longer we were in the *psikhushka*, the more we forgot. A woman died after spending thirty years there. Another got there in 1969; after the treatment that attacked her memory, she couldn't remember what year they had freed her. Nobody remembered dates. Many women went crazy.

"In the *psikhushka*, a person became aware that the regime was totally arbitrary and totally lawless. Nobody could defend you. You couldn't even count on the doctors to be honorable, although they were our only hope. We tried to persuade ourselves that the doctors were our friends; otherwise, we would have been driven to suicide. The fact is that the doctors weren't honorable. They couldn't be. The *psikhushka* was set up to punish us, just that. It was a place where the authorities could get rid of people who were ideologically and politically inconvenient. That's why they fired the honorable doctors and filled the psychiatric centers with obedient pseudo-doctors who were willing to do anything for a bonus.

"Every morning on waking up, a person wondered, 'Have I gone crazy yet? Or am I still normal? I'd say I'm normal, but that's just what crazy people believe.' The worst part of it, what made even the optimists despair, was the fact that nobody knew how long they'd be there, because we hadn't been sentenced. Officially, we were free, we were only 'in treatment.' Nobody knew what they would do to them, nor how it would end.

"In this totally unjust situation, at the mercy of doctors who were puppets of the KGB, after a few months anyone who was sensitive or vulnerable would begin to show signs of mental illness. The most common reaction was constant anguish, the sensation of being persecuted by both the doctors and the other 'patients,' that is, these people would develop a persecution complex and paranoia. It was unspeakably horrible. There's no worse form of torture anywhere.

"What saved me was my conscience. I told myself over and over that I had done what had to be done. Knowing that you've done the right thing, that you've followed the demands of your conscience, is critical. Thanks to that conviction—if you're not given aggressive drugs for too long—you can survive intact.

"They tortured me, but I was at peace with myself. This feeling comes only when you know you've done the right thing.

"I was also saved by the poetry I tried to compose to show myself that I was sane. I was imprisoned in the psychiatric center for a little over two years. In 1972 they freed me, because people abroad had said and written so much about me and the way I had been treated. 'Only two years? That's nothing!' people I knew told me, but when a fellow dissident asked me if I would trade those years for three in the Gulag, I answered, 'I would trade my time in the hospital not just for three, but for seven years in the Gulag!'"

{7}

When they released me from the psychiatric prison, I took up right away with my dissident friends and went back to work. Once again, I became involved in protests, gave interviews to foreign journalists, and organized marches. I was delighted to see that our clandestine journal *A Chronicle of Current Events* was prospering. I had helped found it a little before our Red Square demonstration, and in my absence, my friends had kept it going and even extended its coverage. I began typing the journal up again with multiple copies as samizdat. It only reached a limited circle, but it was still a rebellion against the all-powerful and arbitrary government.

"Our power came from the fact that the Western media transmitted everything we produced. Our protests, proposals, and recommendations, disseminated by radio broadcasts throughout the West, reached millions of ears."

Before her arrest, Natalia had gathered together in a single book the texts of the interrogations of all of the participants in the Red Square protest. Miraculously, she had gotten hold of these reports from the KGB. Her friends smuggled copies out to the West, and the book was published in a number of countries: Great Britain, France, Mexico, and the United States. It's called *Red Square at Noon*. In the introduction to the edition in English, Harrison Salisbury, a journalist for *The New York Times*, writes, "The virtue of this document is its meticulous detail; its crystal exposition of the rude violation of Soviet law: the willful application of force and deceit; the use of the court

as an instrument of injustice; the falsification and suppression
of testimony; the deliberate provocation by state organs; and
over it all the total banality of the system."

Natalia goes on telling her story:

"Because of these actions (the book published in the West,
the clandestine journal, and my constant dissident activity),
the attacks against me continued. The level of persecution
became intolerable. The Soviet authorities let me know that,
like Aleksandr Solzhenitsyn—who had been exiled just a few
years earlier—I was no longer welcome in the Soviet Union.
In September 1975 I was forced into exile in Israel with my
two children."

{8}

A year later, I moved to Paris. Right off I took a liking to
the area where I'd chosen to live, a working-class neighborhood full of immigrants. An exile like them, I was forty
years old and starting a new life.

"A French psychiatric center offered to give me a thorough going-over to see if the chemical treatments I'd been
subjected to in the *psikhushka* had done any lasting damage.
They decided I was fine.

"For the first few months, I devoted every free moment
to exploring Paris. I walked all over to discover what my new
city, and my new life, were like. I loved the cafés, especially the
ones where people played pinball and smoked. I can't imagine

an intellectual life that isn't fueled by cigarettes. Coffee and tobacco keep me alert.

"I've become a real specialist on Paris. The same thing happens in other capitals, like Prague and Warsaw, cities where I've traipsed from one end to another, because I've been invited there, usually to give talks. More than that, they've given me prizes in Prague and Warsaw for having defended their citizens in historic moments when nobody else did anything.

"'Here in Paris, I am part of the editorial committee of different journals, basically run by exiles: *Russkaya Mysl* (Russian Thought) and *Kontinent*. From the beginning of the internet era, I have been an enthusiastic blogger, writing in Russian. There are always many things, serious things, to criticize in Putin's Russia. This is my blog in case you'd like to follow it: ng68.livejournal.com

"I spent thirty years as an exile. Every six months I had to wait in long lines along with other immigrants for them to stamp my passport until, in 2005, Poland offered to make me a citizen, an offer I eagerly accepted. That sort of help can change your life."

{9}

From time to time, I travel to Russia to see what's going on there and to denounce their excesses. In 2011, the Yeltsin Foundation gave me the Russian Prize. In my talk, I recited a

poem I wrote in 1965 and dedicated it to Yuri Galanskov, who
had been jailed for his activism.

In the middle of turbulent darkness,
with a wide smile,
Russia stumbles along
as if it were bumping into a mirror.

"By reading that poem on such a solemn occasion, I
wanted to express the conviction that Russia is still the same
as it was when we knew it as the Soviet Union even though
it has changed its name, its flag, its hymn, and its leader. The
people attending the ceremony understood immediately.

"The Russia I've seen today is notable for a display of gran-
diosity, a rampant acceptance of injustice that touches every
level, the same arbitrary nature that has always characterized
its leaders, and a degree of hypocrisy that I've seen nowhere
else. But, worst of all, it has forgotten its past in a collective
amnesia orchestrated from above. And many people, the majority, obediently accept the obligation to forget what happened before.

"If I go back to Russia from time to time, it is also to attend
the protest marches, including those that commemorate our
first demonstration against the invasion of Czechoslovakia.
Naturally, in Putin's Russia the demonstrators are not looked
upon kindly, but my dissident comrades and I pay no more
attention to the warnings than we did in 1968. We prefer to
be punished than to keep quiet."

{10}

N atalia is not like the women I met who had spent time in the Gulag. They were cordial, moderate, and grateful for my visit and my interest. While I'm walking away from her home and down the breezy street on my way to the metro, I decide that Natalia is the toughest of them all: a determined, tenacious, austere, fierce, and obstinate woman.

{11}

A year later, in 2013, I learned that Natalia Gorbanevskaya had returned to Moscow for the commemoration of the forty-fifth anniversary of the invasion of Czechoslovakia by Soviet troops. There she and the eight other members of that long-ago demonstration had put in an appearance. Once again, the police had arrested them for organizing an unauthorized demonstration.

Three months later, Natalia died in Paris, the city that had provided refuge, but not adopted her. I remembered then that she opened up only to me about her stay in the *psikhushka*, reliving that horrible experience again after so many years. She died in her Paris apartment, surrounded by the papers devoted to her political activities, by her books and her poetry. Up until the end, she worked for her cause tirelessly and, up until that last moment of life, she was sheltered by her world, the world that in times past was the source of both great suffering and great satisfaction.

ULYSSES IN SIBERIA

Janina Misik

{1}

In Ognisko Polskie, the Polish Hearth Club, the main Polish cultural center in London, which is located in a handsome building in Kensington, I am received by a tall, distinguished, white-haired man wearing an elegant suit. When I ask if he knows of any Polish women in London who were confined to the Gulag during the war, he responds immediately: Janina Misik. He telephones her and sets up an appointment for the next morning. Then he invites me to have a coffee in the beautiful restaurant that is part of the cultural center.

{2}

Janina Misik opens the door to me. She is an octogenarian, with white hair tinted a pale blonde, dressed in pants and a sweater the color of fresh peas. While we are still in the doorway, Janina tells me that Zygmunt Sobolewsky, the man who helped me find her yesterday, is thought of very highly by the Poles living in London.

"If you are going to write a book about the Gulag, you need to know his story," she says in a voice that will not take "no" for an answer.

"The thing is: the book I am writing is about women," I point out. "I want to know *your* story, the story of Janina Misik!"

"I'll tell you about myself, but first I want to tell you the story of Zygmunt Sobolewsky. You won't be sorry!"

I realize she is set on doing this. Nothing I say will change her mind, so instead of arguing, I let Janina Misik give me her account as she sees fit.

{3}

The Soviet soldiers burst into the Sobolewsky family home on the night of February 10, 1940. That's what his father told him, since Zygmunt was only two years old at the time. The members of the family had to get dressed as quickly as possible. They were ordered to gather up whatever they might need for the journey. The children were seated on a sleigh, and the parents ordered to drag it—loaded with not just the children but all their baggage as well—to the train station.

"Stalin intended to uproot all the Poles from the Volhynia region and, in fact, all the surrounding territories, the area that in Polish is called *Kresy*, the Outer Limits. Today this area belongs to Belarus and Ukraine. So, under the eyes of the armed Russians, Zygmunt's parents dragged their children over the thick snow for an hour until they reached the nearest station. There the soldiers loaded the family into a cattle car filled with other families. There were no restrooms. The journey to the work camp lasted three weeks. During that time, many people died. There was no food and no heating at a time when the temperature hovered at forty below. The sanitary conditions were unspeakable. They were taken to a camp in the Vologda region. Nothing was there but an enormous forest. They were expected to chop down trees.

"The children who were too young to work attended a Russian school. Zygmunt's brother was one of them. At the school, they were forced to recite a set speech in front of a portrait of Stalin, and the teachers promised that, if they made a good job of it, Stalin would give them candy. 'Pray for Papa Stalin, little one! The good *batushka* will give you candy.' So the little ones recited, and the teacher pulled on a cord and let a couple of candies fall. Zygmunt's brother, who had figured out what was what, did not recite anything, and once he punctured Stalin's eyes in the portrait with a safety pin.

"Zygmunt was suffering from malnutrition. He couldn't walk or even stand upright; he had to lie down. Once in the work camp, a woman gave him a piece of bread, and a man rubbed his weak legs with oil. Even today he remembers how much that helped him. The man was a Siberian shaman.

"As an adult, he knew about the Gulag from what his father had told him, but at home no one could talk about the camps in front of his mother, who suffered from trauma for the rest of her life. After Stalin and the Polish government in London (under Władysław Sikorski) signed a pact to free the Polish prisoners, the family embarked on a journey that would take them from the north of the Soviet Union all the way south, to Uzbekistan. Zygmunt only remembered fragments of the trip, shadows, faceless figures. Traveling through the Soviet Union that winter, the family saw suffering and death wherever they looked. People were dying by the hundreds, and many of the survivors were sent to the Gulag. In that bitter cold, the people who escaped on foot or by sleigh often weren't strong enough for the trip; many of them just collapsed, whether from fatigue or worse. Some resorted to cannibalism. If they had that plan in mind, they took along a victim whom they had already picked and fattened up. When they ran out of food, they devoured the chosen one. All the cadavers lay frozen stiff beside the road. Zygmunt's father pulled his family on a sled for months, over ice and snow. Later he loaded them on a little boat and pulled it by rope down the Volga. Finally, he drove them in a cart over dusty, bumpy roads. In the south, they had to cross a desert.

"The family stayed in Uzbekistan for a little over a year and a half. Zygmunt still couldn't stand up or walk; he was debilitated, exhausted, and his legs just didn't respond. But he would always remember one thing very precisely: one day his brother lifted him up from the kibitka, the windowless mud hut, that was their home. The desert extended as far as his eyes could see, but he could make out a tree in the distance. His brother ran, jumped over a fence, and climbed up that tree to steal an apple, an exceptional treat that the family had not tasted in years and Zygmunt, never. The apple was for him.

"Just as they had in Russia, the family suffered from hunger in Uzbekistan. People made soup out of whatever they could find: turtles, roots, and dogs. Every day produced more deaths: Uzbeks, Poles, Russians... death did not favor any nationality.

"Zygmunt remembers that one day, when he was four years old, the authorities led a group of Poles from the desert of Uzbekistan to the port of Krasnovodsk in Turkmenia, now known as Turkmenistan, that, like Uzbekistan at the time, belonged to the Soviet Union. They took a boat to Persia that was full of people who were fleeing from Stalin. Some of them drowned in the Caspian Sea, because they jumped overboard and swam against the waves, but they couldn't reach the boat again.

"When they reached Persia, they were nothing but skeletons covered in rags. They were taken to the hospital immediately, because every single one of them needed medical attention. After years of starvation and cold, with temperatures that fell as much as fifty degrees below zero, they were debilitated and sick. Tuberculosis, typhoid, and dysentery were the most common ailments. Zygmunt's father, for example, had his boots stolen in the Gulag. It happened often. The Soviet employees took what they wanted from the prisoners. As a result, Zygmunt's father had to wrap his feet in rags to keep from walking directly on the ice. He went to his work as a wood-cutter every day without shoes. After doing this for a while, he lost movement in his feet, because they were frozen.

Zygmunt's brother died in Tehran in 1942. He is buried in the city cemetery, where a big section is set apart for the dead Poles.

"Later they were transferred to Pakistan as political refugees, and there they lived in camping tents in the desert, near Karachi. At night the jackals and the hyenas circled their tent, looking for food. Zygmunt continued to be seriously ill. They took him to the military hospital that was also installed in a tent in the same desert. The patients were primarily English and American soldiers; one of them gave Zygmunt a stuffed bear that would keep him company for a long time. Thanks to the treatment he received there, Zygmunt finally began to walk when he was five years old.

"In December 1943, they sent the Poles to a refugee camp in the south of India, in Kolhapur near Hyderabad. After their long journey, India seemed like paradise. They had enough food, because they received money from the Polish government in exile. There were only two seasons in the south of India: hot and very hot. People who had spent years in the north of Russia appreciated that heat, even the children. Zygmunt has never forgotten how to count in the Telugu language. However, his parents kept asking each other desperately, 'What will become of us? What will become of our children?' They stayed in India for four years. For the first time, the children began going to school. The Poles put together a sort of textbook and organized classes, but the parents continued to suffer from their uncertain situation. 'Will it ever be possible to return to Poland? Where will we live?' Then one day they were ordered to pack up their bundles again.

"After a three-week trip by boat, on September 26, 1947, they reached the English port of Southampton. Zygmunt was nine years old by then. They were taken by truck to a refugee camp, then to another and another. They were moved repeatedly. In the huts, which were shaped like barrels, there was nothing but beds. Whatever belongings they had were stowed under the bed. Once again, however, the Poles improvised schools for the children.

"One day, Zygmunt found himself in a regular English school. He didn't understand anything, and with staring eyes, he looked at the list of subjects he would be taught: algebra, arithmetic, geometry, Latin. These words meant nothing to him. His parents knew no English. In the refugee camps, people spoke Russian, and with each other the family spoke Polish, so the adults had had no chance to learn the language, much less teach it to the children, and yet, in spite of these obstacles, Zygmunt *did* learn English and wound up getting a good job in London."

{4}

Yes, I'm really pleased you told me that story," I answer Janina Misik's question. Then I focus on her own narrative. After the first part, I interrupt her to go over the beginning again:

"I see a schoolgirl with her hair in chestnut pigtails, tied with red ribbons; she carries a leather purse over her shoulder. She's twelve years old. She goes out with her school friends and crosses a square in the city of Rivne in the Volhynia area of eastern Poland. The city boasts a small baroque church. It's lunch time. Everything is quiet; even the church beggar is nodding off. The schoolgirl tries to convince her friends to go swimming in the river with her sister and her: 'Come on. We're taking a big blow-up ball,' she promises.

"Is this right?" I ask to make sure I've understood her correctly.

"Yes, I was the schoolgirl, seventy years ago."

She nods her head slightly several times as if to herself. Clearly, her thoughts have wandered far from the apartment in the south of London where I am paying her a visit and where we have settled down in a sitting room decorated with dolls whose eyes open and close, paper flowers, photographs, and souvenirs of all sorts. The room suggests that the owner has led a rich emotional life. Janina Misik is thinking about the little city with the baroque church and the red roofs, the city from which she was torn so brutally by one of the dictatorships that characterized the twentieth century and deprived her of her childhood.

"On September 17, 1939, the Soviet soldiers captured the city," Janina whispers her words as if she does not want to even say them. She fixes her gaze on the bunch of flowers in a vase on top of the tea table between us. What a wonderful smell! On the way to her house, I had bought her two bunches of violet-colored hyacinths in a little neighborhood shop. With a sigh, she continues, "I remember the hordes of screeching Russians—lots of them drunk—who were laughing at us, the Poles.

"On February 10, 1940, at five in the morning, the Soviet secret police stormed our house, yelling, 'Hands up!' as if we were criminals!" she says the words with a fresh sense of indignation as though it had happened yesterday and not seventy years ago. Still offended, she shakes her head before continuing, "When they saw we were terrified, they lowered their voices a little: *'Sobiraites s veschami!* Get your bags together!' That expression has stayed with me for the rest of my life. My mother didn't get up or even breathe. We thought she had been paralyzed by fear, but that wasn't the problem: she had had a heart attack. My nine-year-old brother looked after her. My father wasn't there. He was half-Jewish, and at that time of mass arrests, he was afraid they would come for him, so he spent his nights in the houses of different friends. My older sister got a message through to him. When he arrived, they had just given us the order to pack up. With his help, my sister and I gathered together as much as they'd let us take.

"I felt an overwhelming, desperate rage. I wanted to strike out at them, but the best I could do was shout. I was nothing but a little girl, and yet I screamed at them: 'What do you plan to do with us? Where did you get the idea that it's all right to burst into an apartment, into the home of people you don't even know at five in the morning? To wake up a family with children? This is *our* home. *We* live here! Don't you see what you've done,' I said, pointing to my mother. She was slowly recovering from the attack, which turned out to be minor.

"They took pity on us and stopped shouting. They helped us pack warm clothes and a little food, basically bread and potatoes. They weren't evil. We loaded Mama and our bags on the sled, and, while the Russians kept an eye on us, we pulled it over the snow up to the train."

{5}

The hyacinths in the vase still give off a sweet smell that is indifferent to the horrors and injustices Janina talks about.

"The trip in a train with nothing but cattle cars lasted two weeks," she continues. "There was, of course, no heat. The cars were packed full, and the communal restrooms were in the middle of one of them. Sometimes we stopped so that people could do their business, always in a crowd and watched over by a policeman with a shotgun. We were not given anything to eat, only hot water. Through the barred window, we could see a snowy landscape, but we had no idea where they were taking us. What I remember about the journey, besides my hunger, was the exhaustion that came from our fear of the future. Mama cried nonstop. It seemed as if she were losing her mind.

"We reached a work camp near the city where Gorky was born; it was called Nizhny Novgorod, both before and after the Soviets. They housed us in wooden huts. Our family of five was assigned a bunk bed. My parents slept on the bottom berth, with my brother, sister, and me on top. We felt as though we were in a cage. The day after we got there, they sent us off to work. We worked fourteen hours a day, chopping down trees, in deep snow, without having the least bit of experience. We were city people. My father had worked in the city government; my mother had been a voracious reader and a good pianist."

The dolls that surround us in Janina's apartment seem to blink their crystal eyes as if in agreement with what she says.

"However," she continues in a much stronger, almost happy, tone of voice, "I have to say that the Russians treated us with consideration. They were almost as bereft as we were. The men had been recruited into the army or condemned to the Gulag. There were also a lot of women there. The Russians encouraged the idea of fraternity between people from the different Slavic countries. They helped us as much as they could. They tried to be hospitable as though we were guests who had come a long way to visit. I'm not talking about the guards, but about the Russians who were condemned like us. The Russians had a hard time. Imagine: I read recently that Stalin had twenty-two million people killed. His daughter, Svetlana, said so. She lived in the United States and could not forgive her father for what he had done.

"My father was a man of deep religious convictions. In the Gulag, he organized gatherings devoted to discussing the Bible, and he could recite whole pages by heart. The administration punished him, because religion was forbidden in the camps. But my father did not pay any attention to them, and he kept on with his gatherings. In the Soviet Union, the country people hid their icons in suitcases under the bed. They were afraid to open them in case their children saw and gave them away. In those days, it was considered good behavior to denounce your parents. Not doing so was itself a reason for punishment.

"The trees we were sawing and chopping down were going to be used for train tracks. We found out that the project had been abandoned, but they still forced us to keep on working. All that suffering had no point. The worst thing was knowing that we were breaking our backs like slaves on work that was absolutely useless. A person can survive many things if there's a goal. Otherwise, it's pure torture.

"We suffered from hunger and cold without a break. We were overwhelmed by sadness. We didn't know what would become of us. The children dreamed about only one thing: having enough bread, eating until we were full. Constant hunger is what I remember most clearly from my childhood. The trauma caused by not having enough food is part of my life, even today. That's why my refrigerator is always full, and I eat more than I should. Even after all these years, I have never lost the fear that at any moment someone might seize the food from my mouth, so I always try to keep my stomach full just in case."

As Janina Misik says this, she looks around as if demanding that the dolls back up what she has said.

{6}

I remember that once my father told us the story of an American who had cut trees with him for a while. He was moved later. I even remember his name: Cy Oggins. Later I tried to find out what had become of him. I've always been interested in how the foreigners in the Gulag ended up. I must have identified with them. This is what happened....

"'I'm Cy' was the way Isaiah introduced himself. His parents were Russian Jews who had found refuge in the United States. They spoke Yiddish at home. They had named their baby Isaiah, Isai in Russian. 'Cy' was an abbreviation.

"Brilliant and curious, he soon became the pride of the family. In the second decade of the twentieth century, his older brother David paid for his studies at Columbia University in New York even though the expense almost ruined him. Cy wanted to be a university professor. Near the end of his studies, he took a job with the Yale University Press. At the university, he saw many cases of social and political injustice, and, since he was young and sensitive, he protested. About that time, he met Nerma, a militant Communist. They got married, and—under his wife's influence—he began to work for the Soviet secret service.

"They sent him first to Berlin. Later he and Nerma moved to Paris. They told him to spy on the Russians who had emigrated there after the Revolution, especially the czar's family, the Romanovs. Different missions took him to China, but he had to leave Nerma and his son Robin behind. After he had been sent to Shanghai several times, the authorities told him to come to Moscow. He spent a few uneasy months there, knowing what such a demand meant, particularly in the second half of the thirties, when Stalin's purges were well underway. To add to his unhappiness, he wanted to rejoin his family who, because of his own warning, had returned to the United States. Europe was on the brink of war.

"Finally, his fears were realized: one freezing cold night in February 1939, the police knocked at his door on the top floor of the Moskva Hotel. He wound up in a detention cell in Lubyanka Prison. On January 5, 1940, he was sentenced, naturally without any chance to present a defense, to eight years of forced labor. They sent him to Norilsk, the northernmost camp of all.

"Two years into his sentence, Cy, who'd never been particularly healthy, was on the point of death. Jacques Rossi, a Frenchman who was with him in Norilsk, got a Polish officer to deliver a letter to the ambassador of the United States: 'Cy Oggins, an American citizen who is in the prison camp Norillag at Norilsk, is in very poor physical condition.' US diplomats immediately asked to see the prisoner. The Soviet authorities sent him back to the Butyrka prison in Moscow to fatten him up so that the diplomats wouldn't see the sorry state he was in.

"In spite of these Soviet efforts, the young American diplomats were shocked to see a forty-two-year-old man who looked twice that age and seemed near death. Cy answered the diplomats' questions. He begged them repeatedly to get in touch with his wife and son. The diplomats wrote to let Washington know what had happened and added that they would intercede, so he could be repatriated.

"On March 4, 1943, Nerma received an official letter from the State Department's assistant chief, Special Division:

My dear Mrs. Oggins:

*I refer to previous correspondence concerning your husband,
Mr. Isaiah Oggins, who is imprisoned in the Soviet Union. The
Department is in receipt of a report from the American Embassy
in the Soviet Union to the effect that the Soviet authorities have
indicated that there will be little delay in releasing your husband
at such time as he is furnished with a passport, it being understood that he would have to be repatriated promptly.*

"Five days later, Nerma received another letter in which
Washington asked her for one thousand and two hundred
dollars to pay for her husband's trip from Moscow to the
United States. In three weeks, Nerma managed to get together four hundred and fifty dollars. She only had a badly
paid, part-time job. At the time she so desperately needed
the twelve hundred dollars she was only earning a hundred a month. Oggins's friends did not help her, because
they viewed her as an extremist. She still believed blindly
in Stalin.

"On June 22, Nerma received a message from the State
Department: 'Competent Soviet authorities have informed
the Embassy that they cannot reconsider your husband's case.
It is therefore impossible to obtain his release at this time.' And
they returned her four hundred and fifty dollars. Moscow had
never intended to liberate him.

"What was happening to Cy in the meantime? His years
of forced labor in a land of perpetual ice and snow with a

constant wind blowing from the North Pole had left him in a desperate state, prematurely aged and physically weak. When they took him to the Butyrka prison in Moscow, where he was interviewed twice by the US diplomats, he took advantage of the opportunity to send two short telegrams to his wife. In the first, he wrote: 'I should appreciate your doing everything you can to make it possible for us to be together again and I am looking forward to that time.' And in the second: 'I urgently request you to make every possible effort to assist me for I need all your help and love.'

"At the beginning of 1947, the eight years to which Cy had been condemned were up. In the summer of that year, they went to his cell and told him that he would be freed. They took him to a laboratory in a building next to the prison. 'It's a mere formality, and after that, you will be free,' they explained. Professor Mairanovsky gave him an injection. Cy began to pant, and then his heart stopped. Oggins's murder was explicitly ordered by Stalin. Nerma did not find out about her husband's death until much later.

"Why didn't Nerma do anything when she knew her husband was in prison? She could have written an article for the newspapers to publicize his case, and the situation would have been resolved. Until her death in 1995 at the age of ninety-seven, Nerma remained a fervent Communist. She never said anything, because if she had admitted that Cy was in the Gulag, she would have had to recognize that her beliefs were mistaken, and her whole life would have lost its meaning."

{7}

While Janina is telling this story, I notice that the walls of her sitting room, like the tables, are covered with framed photographs. To encourage her, I ask Janina if she had made friends in the Gulag.

"People treated us decently, it's quite true, but they were also afraid of us, because we were foreigners. If they developed any kind of relationship with my family, they might have serious problems with the directors of the camp, so we were left to ourselves, alone in a work camp that was isolated in the woods and surrounded by ice and snow. For a little while I had a Polish friend, but she wasn't there long.

"Later the political situation changed. Hitler attacked Poland, which was one of the Allied Powers, and the Polish prime minister, Władysław Sikorski, who was exiled in London, got Stalin to free the Poles in Russian captivity; however, when he asked the International Red Cross to investigate the massacre of Polish officers in Katyn, Stalin suspended diplomatic relations with our country. We couldn't go home, then, but after almost two years in the Siberian Gulag, in 1940—thanks to Sikorski's diplomatic maneuvering—they sent us to the south of the Soviet Union."

Janina pronounces the prime minister's name with a respect and gratitude that are touching, a response to Sikorski's help shared by other Polish exiles from that generation.

"We reached Uzbekistan," Janina continues. "We traveled there much like Zygmunt Sobolewsky's family: in summer, we used a small boat on the Volga; in winter, when snow covered everything and the river and lakes were frozen solid, we relied on a sled that one of us had to drag. We covered part of the route by train, but more than anything we walked. We traveled about four thousand kilometers. When we reached Uzbekistan, we were skin and bones, and those bones creaked. We looked like the survivors of a Nazi concentration camp, just as they've been shown in countless photographs. Almost everyone in our group was sick. Others had died of malnutrition. Many who reached Uzbekistan had come out of the prisons in Moscow, where they'd been tortured. The man I would marry, another Pole, had been in Lubyanka.

· "In Uzbekistan, we lived in the middle of the desert in a camping tent or in a kibitka, a mud hut without windows that we built ourselves from the earth under our feet. The Uzbeks lived the same way. In winter it snowed and froze over, but we didn't have stoves. Life in the desert was primitive. There were medieval Uzbek cities in the oases, but these were far away. It goes without saying that we didn't see mythic cities like Samarkand or Bukhara, which lay on the Silk Road. That was forbidden.

"The desert water was contaminated. You couldn't drink it, and the children were always thirsty. That's why so many of them died from poisoning. And the ones who didn't die, suffered from typhoid or dysentery. Hunger was unrelenting. If I had to define my childhood, I'd use one word: 'hunger.'

"We didn't have beds. We slept on top of blankets on the floor. There were no hospitals nearby. One morning I woke up to find my best friend lying dead. I was inconsolable, but I had to accept the loss, because death was the order of the day.

My sister contracted typhoid and was sick for a long time, but she was young. She got well, and she's still alive. She lives in Birmingham now and is eighty-six years old.

"How did I survive it all? Perhaps thanks to the hope our suffering would not last forever and, eventually, better times would come. That totally illogical sense of hope has never left me."

{8}

Those of us who weren't sick worked in the cotton fields, which were quite a distance away. They paid us with flour. In the morning, we walked for hours until we got there. At night, we walked home. Always starving and dead tired, we were paid for how much we had done, but we could never reach our quota. Yet people were kind to us. So kind!"

Janina holds her arms out as if she wanted to embrace— perhaps not the whole universe—but at least the world of her dolls, who look at her expectantly without blinking.

"At night the Uzbek families invited us to sit down with them. They were almost as poor as we were, but they invited us to share the little they had. We sat in front of their kibitka on a mattress, covered with rugs or blankets, the men wearing colored caps, the women with cotton skirts, in bright patterns, that brushed the ground, and we drank green tea with them from blue and white porcelain bowls. They served us bread with the tea, and occasionally offered us chewy sweets shaped into little balls or rolls."

{9}

The Poles organized schools in the Uzbek desert. People in very different fields taught the classes. The children, both boys and girls, worked only a few days of the week; the rest of the time was set aside for class. In the end, we got a fairly decent education. We studied mathematics, physics, history, language, music theory, Polish spelling, world literature, and even drawing. When we didn't have any paper, we drew on the blackboard or even on the desert sand. We had an excellent English teacher, who used that language with us right from the start. That was his method. Later, for everyone who survived and moved to London, it proved to be invaluable.

"After a year and a half in the desert, they deported us to the mountains of Uzbekistan, near the little city of Kitab. Oddly, *kitab* means book in the local language. No matter where we looked there, we saw natural wonders: valleys and rivers, fields and forests, tall mountains with their peaks covered in snow. And sometimes we even managed to trade bread and rice for fruit. In Kitab, there was also a Polish cemetery, because people kept on dying.

"Later we moved to the port of Krasnovodsk in Turkmenistan and from there by boat to Pahlev in Persia. I remember the moment we arrived: the boat drew up to a beautiful, green land. We were all filled with hope, and our hopes were fulfilled, because in Persia the United Kingdom extended its protection and aid. That's what General Sikorski had worked out with the English. The Persians, who were much richer than the Uzbeks, took great care of us. The sick were sent to the hospital. Since we were nothing but bones, we were given great quantities of food. Most of the adults worked in factories. The children attended a school where the teachers were Poles. At first, we lived in special residences with many people crowded in each room. Later on, they moved us to different cities in Palestine, including Nazareth, and then finally to Lebanon and Egypt. By that time, I was a teenager, and the entire trip seemed like a fabulous adventure.

"My big sister stayed in Lebanon for a while with our mother, who—after going hungry for years—had become so weak that she could no longer stand up. My sister took charge of her. An English officer whom my sister had met in Tehran looked after both of them. He just couldn't live without my sister. He stayed by her side during the rest of our hard journey. He even learned Polish and also learned to cook special Polish dishes. He called my sister his "Polish rose." They got married later in England. Every Sunday he served her breakfast in bed and always made sure there was a fresh rose on the tray!"

{10}

Janina realizes that I've been looking at a small black-and-white photograph in a gold-leaf frame that stands out on the wall. It shows a group of carefree girls mounted on a camel.

"I was sixteen when the picture was taken. We were in Palestine. They also treated us very well there."

I ask her if during their exodus the family ever expected to return to Poland. Janina shakes her head.

"After the Yalta agreement, in which the United States and the United Kingdom ceded Poland and other central European countries to the Soviet Union, we saw very clearly that we couldn't go home. We had experienced communism in Russia, and we knew we didn't want to live under that kind of regime no matter what. Worse yet, the part of Poland my family came from now was actually part of the Soviet Union. We had more than enough reasons for refusing to go back to what would be a hell. That's when they sent us to Egypt, where we lived in the desert, just as we had in Uzbekistan. Finally, in 1947, they put us on a boat in Port Said and sent us to Southampton. After so many years in the desert, it was wonderful to see a green landscape even though we had to live at first in a refugee camp.

"I was young. I knew that I wanted to live a full life, to have a worthwhile job, and to be useful. I realized that I'd need a university degree to do that, so I enrolled at the University of Guildford. I got a degree in teaching and found work at the British Council as an interpreter and organizer of cultural events. Through my work, I met people from all over the world. It was a stimulating and exciting job.

"In England, I met the man I would wind up marrying. He was also Polish, an officer in the army and a painter. We had a son we named Alec. He's sixty years old now. My first husband died of cancer in 1990. My second husband had been seriously injured in Italy during the war, and he suffered from post-traumatic stress. He died a year ago due to a mixture of dementia and Alzheimer's, the cruelest disease of all. But life goes on. Now, I spend my time organizing gatherings of Poles in a center across from my home. Do you have time? Do you want me to take you there for lunch? What? You're leaving England today? All right, but at least we can have a coffee and a Polish pastry. Why not? Not just a coffee? You make me feel I'm a very bad hostess. All right. It looks like I can't convince you.

"Now I've lost track.... Oh, yes, my husband with Alzheimer's. I never guessed I'd have to take care of someone with such a terrible illness, but when there was no choice, I found the strength to do it. A person can put up with much more than you'd think. It's a lesson I learned from life at a very young age. If you want to get something out of this life, you have to fight for it, no matter what stands in your way, so I keep on organizing cultural activities as I did before, and I'm happy to do something for others. Being useful is the greatest satisfaction of all. I also take care of children with mental disabilities. Do you see them here? In the photograph? There are people in Poland who contribute on their own behalf or in the name of an organization. Most of the donations are modest. People give what they can. And once a week I organize a gathering here at home with tea, music, and recitals. I know you're leaving today, but the next time you're in London, you must come!

"Before my death, I want to do more good things. When I die, I don't want to stand before God with empty hands, you see? I want to give other people what politics and history deprived me of in my childhood."

Janina Misik finishes her cappuccino. She is like a feminine, modern-day Ulysses, who after much wandering has finally found her Ithaca in the Polish community of London.

"I can never thank the English enough for giving us the chance to save our lives and sharing what they had, whether it was a lot or a little." She sighs, and her happy gaze drifts off into the mist of long-ago memories.

ARIADNE, DAUGHTER OF THE LABYRINTH

Galya Safonova

{1}

Galina Stepanovna Safonova—Galya to her friends—is younger than the other women I have interviewed, because she was not arrested or sentenced to the Gulag; instead, she was born in a camp in the north of Russia, in the 1940s. Since the barracks the child had shared with her mother and other women prisoners, the watch tower and the barbed wire fencing were all she had ever known, Galya accepted them all without question—like the guard dogs, which were always tethered unless someone tried to escape—as well as the rage, desperation, and depression of her surroundings.

We sit down at her table, each of us with a cup of strong, sweet tea as the Russians like it. Then Galya begins telling her story.

{2}

As soon as she graduated from the School of Medicine in Moscow, my mother, who was named Tamara and was an epidemiologist, started work at the hospital," Galya says in a resolute voice. She must have prepared an outline ahead of time. "Then she was admitted into the well-known Mechnikov Institute. It was there that she became interested in microbiology, since epidemiology and microbiology are related sciences. While she was studying at the Mechnikov, which was also a research center, she continued working, and she got married and had two children, my older siblings, a girl and a boy. They were born in 1929 and 1930, respectively."

According to Galya, in the meantime, strange things began happening in the Far East: people were dying in the villages for unknown reasons. Since they were peasants, the authorities didn't care about their deaths, that is, until the epidemic spread to the soldiers in the Red Army who were serving in that area. When the soldiers began to die, the defensive capacity of the country was in danger. Kliment Voroshilov, the Defense Minister, signed an order to send an expedition of Moscow doctors to the Far East to discover the cause of the plague. The group was led by Lev Aleksandrovich Zilber and was made up of seven investigators. Galya's mother was one of the epidemiologists on the expedition.

The members of the group traveled to the east and spent almost a year there. After the first six months, they managed to uncover the cause of the deaths—a disease they dubbed taiga encephalitis, so named because it was spread by ticks in the swampy, boreal forests: the taiga. Once their mission was accomplished, they could go home. But Zilber, the head of the expedition, was a tenacious researcher and he proposed that they come up with an antidote, which took six more months of experimentation.

"Which experiments did they get involved in?" I ask.

"A number of the team members," narrates Galya, "offered to be guinea pigs: they were inoculated with the bacteria and then treated. This decision had consequences: a certain Soloviov suffered from facial paralysis. After returning to Moscow, he managed to finish his graduate studies and become an academic. The expedition returned to the capital in triumph, with an antidote in hand. The team members were praised and rewarded with vacations in state-owned spas.

"The members of the expedition, including my mother, who were too busy with work to go on vacation were forced to witness a shocking development: can you imagine that the NKVD, our secret police, had initiated a lawsuit against Zilber, on the basis of some presumed denunciations, for crimes against the Russian people! The members of the expedition who had stayed in Moscow were pressured to sign an unfounded accusation against him. My mother refused. In the meantime, agents of the NKVD had seized the documentation related to the expedition, so that the members had no proof of their leader's innocence. The inhuman nature of the regime was very clear from the way they treated those blameless people who represented the very best of the nation's cultural and intellectual life. They put them in cattle cars and sent them off to the Gulag. In a cruel joke of fate, their destination was named Svobodni, which means 'Free.'"

{3}

In the Gulag, Galya's mother continued to practice medicine. After some time she was transferred to another camp where the doctor had just died and Galya's mother was needed there to take his place. The first thing she did was visit the infirmary. She talked to the patients and studied their clinical files, since she had to decide if they were strong enough for heavy work like chopping down trees in that hostile climate. It became also part of her duties to approve a special diet for patients who suffered from serious stomach problems, like ulcers. Galya's mother found that the ones being treated with this diet were healthy. They were common criminals who enjoyed a position of privilege in the Gulag. People who didn't form part of their fraternity were dying, but nobody cared. The political prisoners in the infirmary were rotting away, and no one could even be bothered to feed them.

Galya's mother decided to change things in that infirmary. She examined one of those criminal impostors and told him that he was fit for the hardest work. He threatened to stab her, and he almost carried out his threat, but the doctor was not cowed. She hit him on the hand that held the knife, and it fell. The male nurses stepped in and held him down. Later, he was transferred to another camp.

Galya sips her tea and continues:

"Since the news began to get out that my mother was a very good doctor, she was asked to take care not just of the prisoners, but also of sick people from villages and towns in the area. Up there, in the taiga beyond the Arctic Circle, the distance between settlements was enormous. One of the military units posted there gave my mother a horse named Boy so that she could get around more easily. That horse had a mind of his own. Once, when my mother was going to a place that was fairly close, she decided to ride instead of taking the cart. When she rode by the military barracks, they were training their horses to jump. My mother was unfamiliar with Boy's military training. As soon as he smelled his mates, he made up his mind to join them and took off at a gallop. He flew over every hurdle that had been set up for the exercise and kept on going. On the basis of that anecdote, the news spread that, in addition to being an excellent doctor, my mother was also a kind of Amazon. She became a real celebrity."

{4}

In the meantime, around 1940, the scientist Zilber was freed. He immediately began to make efforts to liberate my mother and another member of the expedition. Just when Zilber had set to work gathering the documentation he needed, the war started. They locked him up again in 1942.

"My mother wound up in the Arkhangelsk area, in Kotlas, where I was born. Earlier she had tried to sign up as a volunteer at the front, surely in hopes of joining my father, who was stationed there.

"My maternal grandparents were also doctors. When my grandmother died, my mother was small, and an aunt in Moscow took her in: Yulizavera Dudina, an actress in the famous Moscow Art Theater. Her husband was a painter and a member of the Fine Arts Academy in Russia. They lived on Arbat Street. Now old enough to form a family, my mother was planning to marry Vladimir Bazhenov, a recently graduated surgeon, the firstborn son of a famous family of artists in Moscow. Vladimir had a sister and five brothers, one of whom—Aleksandr—was a painter and well known for his harum-scarum ways. Three of the brothers, including Aleksandr, were in love with my mother, but it looked as though the oldest, Vladimir, had won her over. The two of them had even picked a date for the wedding, but suddenly a radical change took place, and my mother wound up marrying Aleksandr. All of that happened before my mother met the man who would be my father."

{5}

Galya was born in 1942 at the Kotlas work camp. Her birth was entered in the Gulag register at Pechora, in the Arkhangelsk area, in the north of Russia. At that time, although her mother enjoyed a certain degree of freedom, she lived and worked in the Gulag. Galya's earliest memories go back to when she was four. She remembers the barracks, which were connected by a covered walkway made out of simple wooden boards. Galya and her mother lived in one of them, and the other was the so-called House of Culture, a place devoted to Communist propaganda and reeducation. The kitchen was there too.

Galya brings out a chocolate bar on a plate from the kitchen. As she deposits it on the table between us, she recalls her childhood in the Gulag.

"When I was five, they freed my mother from the camp but did not allow her to return home. They forced her to stay near the Kotlas camp, where she was working as an epidemiologist in a hospital. They provided us with a minuscule room—a cubicle, really—with just enough space to sleep, in a residence for railroad workers. I remember a long, long hallway, with rooms on each side. There was a little kitchen that everyone shared and that doubled as a laundry room. In spite of all the drawbacks, my mother never became resentful or embittered.

"I remember a funny story. When we moved from the Gulag to the village next door, I was surprised to see dogs running loose. Up until that time, I'd only seen the guards' dogs, which were always chained. I had thought of dogs as animals that only lived on chains.

"In my eyes the rage, the desperation, and the depression all around me also seemed perfectly natural. We had a neighbor who was constantly stirring up trouble. He particularly liked to knock women around. When he went too far, my mother was the person who almost always calmed things down. She came running to the aid of anyone who was being mistreated, no matter whether she was involved or not."

{6}

Near the Kotlas camps, in the middle of the woods, they built a stop for the train from Solvychegodsk, which was joined to the station at Kotlas by a narrow-gauge track and a local train. The prisoners from the Gulag built that railroad. In Solvychegodsk, they assigned the mother and daughter a little house in the Finnish style with two main rooms that had a small kitchen with a wood fire and a tiny storage room. The toilet was outside, thirty meters from the house.

"During the winter, we did our business inside in a bucket to keep from going outside in the cold. In that climate, the temperature could easily drop to fifty degrees below zero.

"To survive, my mother raised a pig, then a she-goat; later she added a billy goat and they had kids. We bought the pig in the spring, and we fattened it up until the end of the fall when it was slaughtered. That's how we had food to get us through the winter. My mother was almost never at home, and I—just a little girl—had to take care of the animals. In spite of living in Solvychegodsk, which at that time was made up of four tiny houses in the middle of the woods, my mother kept on working as the doctor of the Kotlas Gulag. I went to a kind of nursery there with other children, most of them produced by the rapes that were so frequent in the labor camps. I didn't find out about that until later."

To get to and from the camp, mother and daughter took a *kukushka*, a "baby buggy," meaning a narrow-gauge train. The machinist, who knew them from all their trips, would salute them by blowing the horn. If he had to wait for them, he'd do it without complaining. Both had a good relationship with him. They never locked the door of their house even though all around them the prisoners, many of them common criminals, were doing construction work. The construction workers knew that their house was open and that Galya's mother always left a bit of food for them, usually potatoes or bread. They'd reciprocate by cutting wood for them and keeping their oven lighted, so when they got home at night, the house was warm and there was a potato casserole ready to eat.

Galya takes a piece of chocolate:

"All in all, I can't say my childhood was unhappy. Considering my young age, I couldn't possibly have realized the kind of situation we were living in. It was all I knew, so I just accepted it as normal.

"I remember the camp was monitored by armed guards who kept an eye on everything from their towers. There were also guards who made rounds. Their presence didn't bother me. Sometimes I even chatted with them. In summer, friends of mine came, daughters of other doctors, and we would go swimming in the river. We also went to the woods to hunt for mushrooms, which my mother used for soup. In the winter, she would marinate cabbage in a barrel. In September we picked blueberries to make compotes and preserves that we would also consume in the winter.

"When we had she-goats, we were never short of milk. I learned to milk them when I was very young. For fodder, I had to gather fifty bundles of birch branches a day. Birch keeps very well during the winter. I did this in the summer.

Since the birch branches are very flexible, it's hard to break them. On the other hand, alder is much more brittle, and the branches break easily. When I realized that, I decided to fool my mother by substituting alder for birch. That way I finished my work much faster. My mother found out and reproached me in no uncertain terms for putting my comfort ahead of our goats' wellbeing. Once they were cut, the alder branches soon became inedible and turned into sawdust. Even today I remember how ashamed I felt when my mother reprimanded me. I loved her, because she was all I had."

{7}

As far as Galya's father goes, that subject was taboo. Mother and daughter never talked about him until Galya was eleven years old.

"My mother traveled often for her work, so I spent a lot of time home alone. Since I was curious, I liked to peer into things. Once I found a little bundle, a kerchief tied at its four corners with something inside. There were a few faded photos of a man and a few letters folded in a triangle, which had come from the front. I read them and realized they were from my father. He addressed both my mother and me very tenderly. My mother didn't want to talk about him. When she did, she always kept it short, saying that he had fought the enemy and that kind of thing. Later I found out that all the correspondence that came in from the front was censored, so you couldn't say very much about what was really happening.

In one of those letters, dated at the end of 1944, my father promised that he would see us soon and bring us presents. Towards the end of the war, he was wounded in the shoulder. It happened in Czechoslovakia. They took him to several different hospitals. My mother repeated over and over that my father had been killed in the war."

{8}

Galya's mother was a great reader, and every time she traveled she came home with books by classic authors, which were hard to find in that environment; the only ones normally available were songs of praise for the Soviet regime.

"I also remember that the women prisoners who worked close to our house made little books for me by hand with their own drawings, dolls too. My favorite doll had a face that looked as though it were made of porcelain although there was, of course, no porcelain at the camp. I don't know how they managed that effect. She had real hair. I still have her. Another doll, a tiny one, was made from bread crumbs and painted in different colors.

"My mother was also good with her hands. Once she made me a dress out of the rags they used in the Gulag to wrap around their feet—socks were forbidden—so that their boots would fit. She and her friends made me the books I've told you about. This shows how hard my mother and the other prisoners worked to provide me with some sense of culture in an atmosphere where there was nothing. It's impressive that people like her, deprived of their liberty in the most atrocious way, preserved their dignity and refused to accept the barbarity that surrounded them, making every effort to transmit their knowledge and culture from one generation to another."

{9}

Concerned because I look tired after my long trip from Chicago to Moscow, Galya gives me another very hot tea and covers my shoulders with a woolen shawl. She waits to see if I am comfortable before returning to her story.

"In spite of having been raised in the Gulag and surely because I had known no other life, my childhood seemed normal to me. I had presents on special days, sang with my mother—even arias from operas. The prisoners—and former prisoners who were obliged to live near the Gulag—taught me to read and to draw. It was a rich life compared to the insipid existence of many people with much greater resources."

For the New Year's celebration—it was prohibited to celebrate Christmas—they always had a tree decorated with ornaments they made themselves, hand-painted pinecones and pretty objects made from the tinfoil they kept from candies. They also hung little king cakes and tangerines, whose odor Galya still associates with New Year's Eve. If occasionally they had fruit to eat, it was because former prisoners sent it to them from the Soviet republics in Central Asia as a way of thanking Galya's mother for her help. Otherwise, there was almost no fruit in the camp. On top of the tree, instead of the Communist red star, they always positioned a little figure of a heron with white wings perched on one foot that a prisoner had made for them.

"We loved each other very much—I've never doubted that—but we didn't treat each other tenderly, perhaps because of the harshness of life at the time, which was even worse around the Gulag. We never used fond nicknames with each other, for example. I only learned to show affection with my children and grandchildren. My mother had given me an authoritarian education. She told one of my aunts that she had had me to give some meaning to her life, because at one point she had lost the will to live. She had me in order to survive, I'd say, but she never told me so. I don't think she was entirely aware of how complicated her life would be as a single mother. That explains why she was often hard on me. I remember, when I was in the nursery, a boy asked me to say out loud without thinking the name of Stalingrad without pronouncing the 'r.' I did what he asked, and it came out 'Stalin gad,' which means 'Stalin is a shit.' My mother was called to the nursery and told off in no uncertain terms. Later she severely punished me.

"In general, my mother avoided talking about the reprisals that had led to her unfortunate situation. She probably was hoping to forget what had happened. The only time she spoke about the subject openly was in front of a camera, six months before her death. When the recording ended, she was running a high fever."

{10}

Galya was eleven years old when Stalin died in early March 1953. After his death, the process of rehabilitating the victims of reprisals got underway. Galya's mother had started writing letters several years earlier to different institutions, including the Office of the Prosecutor General and the Supreme Soviet of the USSR, asking them to review her legal situation: even though she had been "freed," she was still under surveillance and confined in the Kotlas area. Since she worked in an infirmary for the prisoners who built the railroad lines, she had the right to one free train trip a year. Galya was still school age and didn't need a ticket. That's how they traveled to Moscow. In the capital, they stayed with Galya's aunt Yelizaveta on Arbat Street. When Yelizaveta died in 1955, Galya's mother went back to the capital. She filled out paperwork and got hold of a certificate that showed she had been condemned illegally and had been totally rehabilitated. She never received an official apology. She never complained, though. While she was detained, she worked tirelessly. She never stopped fighting to preserve her dignity.

{11}

Once Galya's mother had gotten her certificate of rehabilitation in Moscow, she moved to the capital and worked as a translator from French to Russian for the Mechnikov Institute. Her daughter came with her; Galya was fourteen.

"Life was very different in Moscow. To get to school, I had to catch a bus in Tekstilshchiki, where we were living on the outskirts of town. It left me at a train station. From there I caught a train to Kursk, which was closer in. From Kursk I took the metro to the Kiev station, and from there, finally, I took a trolley to Kutuzovsky Avenue, which is a good neighborhood now, but back then was a slum with its share of garbage dumps. Because of my complicated itinerary, I always got to class late. The chemistry teacher was the only one who didn't let me in the classroom after the bell. We didn't hit it off. She had taken against me. In the tenth grade, I came down with diphtheria; I was very worried about missing too many classes, especially chemistry, because I was struggling with it. However—to the teacher's great surprise—I passed that course with a high grade.

"In contrast, the literature teacher, Anna Feodorovna Zelmanova, was an angel. One time she asked me about my personal situation. She told me to come to her office after class, and she made me write a letter to Khrushchev, explaining the hard circumstances my mother and I faced. The letter began: 'Dear Nikita Sergeyevich: I want to study.'

"Two weeks later they gave me an appointment at the Soviet in Moscow, the city hall of the capital. I remember that it was winter and that I climbed the carpeted stair of the building in *valenki*, the felt boots that country people wore. I came to an enormous office with huge windows and desks covered with baize. A woman was sitting at one of them, looking at two pages from a school notebook. I recognized the letter I had written and saw that a lot of it was underlined in red.

Thanks to my teacher's help, even though it was short, the letter was carefully written, without any padding. Every line made its point."

Two weeks later mother and daughter were provided with a room in a communal apartment, a *kommunalka* on Kutuzovsky Avenue. Although they had to live with many other people and share the kitchen and the only toilet with them, it was a huge improvement. Galya was proud of herself, since it was thanks to her letter, and not her mother's efforts, that they managed to have their own space in Moscow. Galya says: "I am sure they dismissed my mother's petitions, because she was a former prisoner."

{12}

After Galya reached adulthood, she started working as a public relations officer in a government company and occasionally got permission to travel to other countries in the Communist orbit—Bulgaria, Czechoslovakia, and East Germany—to participate in conferences in defense of peace. After her husband sought refuge in the United States, the KGB got in touch with her. She had to list the reasons for his emigration. She explained that he had made the decision himself as an autonomous adult without any advice from her. But she was not allowed to travel abroad until the beginning of perestroika. "In a way," she concludes, "I repeated my mother's experience. She was detained in a camp, and I was detained in the prison that was the USSR."

{13}

Galya's story comes to an end, and we make an appointment for another day. She fixes lunch for the two of us and then shows me her treasures: the dolls and the books that were made for her by the prisoners in the camp. She has never let them go. I pick up one of the books: *Little Red Riding Hood*, with pages in different shapes and sizes, sewn by hand. On each page there are drawings made with colored pencils: Red Riding Hood with her basket of presents, the wolf with the grandmother, Red Riding Hood with the wolf in his disguise. The text of the story is written in ink.

"Each one of these books made me so happy!" Galya exclaims. "When I was a little girl, these were the only form of culture I had. Look, I've kept them all my life! They are my greatest treasure."

EURYDICE IN THE
UNDERWORLD

Irina Emelyanova

{1}

I rina Emelyanova receives me in her apartment in Paris. She is the daughter of Olga Ivinskaya, Boris Pasternak's last love and the inspiration for Lara, the character in *Doctor Zhivago*.

"Shall we sit in the kitchen?" Irina invites me.

I agree, a little perplexed, but then remember the Russian custom of visiting with friends in the kitchen. During the decades of communism, the Russians retired to the kitchen when they needed to talk about delicate matters or share confidences that were not intended for the hidden microphones the secret police installed in the apartments of suspected dissidents. I show my enthusiasm about the idea of having a tête-à-tête in the kitchen.

While she is preparing tea and offering me Russian poppy-seed cookies, Irina starts to speak, slowly and deliberately, as though she were caressing each subject.

{2}

D o you want me to tell you the story of my grandmother? That was my initiation into the world of horror."

Since I am eating a cookie, I just nod my head in agreement.

"Our family was living in a small apartment in Moscow. There were five of us: my grandparents, my mother, my brother, and I. In July 1941, a month before Germany declared war on Russia, the police showed up at our home. They had an order for the arrest of my grandmother Marusia, known by her friends as 'beautiful Marusia,' and they took her to prison."

"But why?" I ask.

"Someone had denounced her. The denunciation was based on a lie, like so many of them at the time. It was probably inspired by a desire to get hold of our apartment. Having an apartment to yourself, without having to share space with who knows how many other residents, was a luxury back then.

"I was three years old when the trial took place, and my grandmother looked a little thinner than usual, but still beautiful. She was calm; she knew she had an excellent lawyer. Her confidence was well placed: the lawyer defended his client brilliantly, as I learned later. Thanks to his help, my grandmother was sentenced to what everybody called jealously 'a punishment fit for a child': six years of forced labor in a camp.

"Later my mother, Olga Ivinskaya, told me that the horrors of war, in spite of the constant hunger and the threat of death, were a blessing compared to the dangers of the totalitarian regime, that reign of deceit, mendacity, and arbitrary punishment.

"At the beginning, my family received the letters that my grandmother Marusia sent from the work camp, but then her messages stopped coming. In the spring of 1943, rumors spread that the German troops were bombing the camps. Olga was afraid for her mother. Despite her efforts, she couldn't find out where Marusia was. Finally, she followed her intuition and set off in search of my grandmother. She didn't have a valid address or even a train ticket (she couldn't afford one because of the poverty caused by the war). On the trains, when the ticket collector came by, the other passengers hid Olga under the seats and covered her with their bundles. No one hurt her; once they heard her story, they treated her with kindness, giving her bread and a place to rest.

"Olga traveled to the work camp where she believed her mother had been sent. Along the way, she encountered real privation. Many people told her that a lot of the camps had been shut down. By pure chance, Olga found her mother close to the camp, coming out of a forest. The once 'beautiful Marusia' was dirty and covered in rags. She was leaning on a twisted stick and looked almost savage. The camp had been closed, and the prisoners had taken off, hiding in the woods, fearful of being trapped and returned to their executioners. They lived on grass, raw mushrooms, and tree bark. Later my grandmother told us that she had even come across cases of cannibalism.

"When my grandmother appeared in our Moscow apartment covered in foul, reeking rags, her hair like a scrubbing brush, and a tree branch in her hand, I started screaming in horror. I thought I was seeing the wicked witch out of a fairy tale. My grandfather, who was wild with joy at her return, tried in vain to persuade me to hug her, because she loved me so much, but for more than a week, I hid every time I caught sight of her."

{3}

Irina serves me more tea and, little by little, as if she were afraid of her own memories and wants to turn them over in her mind before sharing, she starts telling the story of her mother, who had an intimate relationship with the writer Boris Pasternak.

"In 1946, when he was fifty-six, Pasternak met my mother, a poet and translator, in the editorial office of *Novy Mir*, the literary journal she worked for. She was thirty-three at the time. The first phase of the love story between a man in his second marriage, who had fathered two sons, and a divorced woman, who was the mother of two small children, each one the product of a different marriage, took place in Moscow's parks. For months, the lovers recited their poems to each other under the statues of Pushkin and Mayakovsky. No one seemed to pay them any attention, except for the secret police who saw everything and knew everything. Their reaction came soon enough.

"One night in 1949, the police knocked at our door. They searched the apartment, arrested my mother, who was pregnant with Pasternak's child, and took her to prison. The authorities wanted to send us to a boarding school, but thanks to the pressure my grandparents exerted and to Pasternak's promise of economic help, they gave in and let us stay at home.

"By arresting my mother, they were sending the poet a warning. That's the way they operated when it came to writers with a reputation in the West. When Marina Tsvetaeva and her family returned to the USSR from Paris, her husband was tortured to death in prison and her daughter, Ariadna Efron, spent years in the Gulag. Something very similar happened to the first and second husbands, as well as the son, of the poet Anna Akhmatova.

"When Pasternak met Olga, he was starting to write *Doctor Zhivago*, his most ambitious novel. It shows that he was head over heels in love. In the second half of the book, he seems to lose interest in characters like the mysterious Antipov/Strelnikov and Mrs. Zhivago, modeled on his second wife, Zinaida. They fade from sight while Lara, the character inspired by Olga, grows more and more prominent in the narrative until she becomes the protagonist, along with Yuri Zhivago, Pasternak himself.

"In prison, Olga showed great bravery. In spite of the physical and psychic tortures inflicted on the prisoners, she revealed nothing about Pasternak. The authorities decided to go further in their efforts to break down the woman who was so close to a writer the regime considered noxious, because he didn't follow the Soviet canon of socialist realism.

"My mother knew that her friend had a heart condition and had been taken to the hospital. One day her jailers announced that they would let her see Boris. They led her, a pregnant woman, through a labyrinth of subterranean passageways until they finally admitted her to a depository for cadavers. Olga tried to figure out which of the dead figures was Pasternak, but she did not uncover him. The depository was freezing, and since there were no chairs, she sat down on the cement floor and fainted. They took her to the prison hospital, and there the doctor announced that because of her nervous state she had had a miscarriage."

Irina serves me the tea she has prepared. First, she drizzles a few drops of a thick, almost black liquid into my cup and then adds hot water. She offers me sugar. The tea is aromatic, sweet, and strong. Irina tastes it too and smiles, "But that's not everything, not by a long shot!

"At that point, they sent Olga to a forced labor camp," she tells me. "My grandfather could not bear for his daughter to be imprisoned in a camp. He fell sick and died soon after. That was in 1952. The only ones left in the apartment were my brother and I, neither of us even adolescents yet, and our grandmother. During my mother's absence, Boris Pasternak sent us money regularly. We survived only thanks to his help. On a cold day in January, the three of us buried our grandfather and husband in a little tomb, accompanied by a few of his old friends.

"A few months later, my grandmother came home with the news that Pasternak had just had a heart attack. 'What will become of us?' we wondered. He was well known for sharing with friends who had less than he. His friend Ariadna Efron insisted that the writer felt guilty for two reasons: because he had not stopped her mother Marina Tsvetaeva from leaving her exile in Paris to return to Moscow, where agents of the

KGB drove her to suicide, and because he had not put up a better defense of Osip Mandelstam when Stalin called Pasternak on the phone to extract information on his writer friend.

"I'm convinced, however, that Pasternak's generosity was not related to any sense of guilt. It was rooted in his character. From his hospital bed, he kept writing messages to make sure the money he had promised Olga's family would still reach us, so my brother and our grandmother and I managed to stay afloat.

"Pasternak recuperated, although he could no longer make it up to the sixth floor where we lived. That's why he and I—a ten-year-old then—started meeting on the benches of the boulevards of Moscow. That was when I not only lost my fear of the famous man but began to see him as part of the family. Even today I remember the background of those meetings: the noise of the streetcars that passed both ways, the clear sky we saw in the opening between the two rows of tall buildings, and his constant smile."

As Irina says this she smiles too.

"After he recovered, Pasternak began writing to Olga again. He sent letters, and postcards even more, because letters did not always reach their destination. Since only family members had the right to send mail to political prisoners, he always signed, 'Love, Mama.' His missives probably didn't fool anyone: they were characterized by his poetic turn, his amorous enthusiasm and, sometimes, his sense of desperation—but, then, in seventeenth-century France, Madame de Sévigné sent her daughter, who was living in Paris, letters that could compete with the most poetic love letters."

{4}

I still haven't told you that, after her miscarriage, my mother had a summary trial and was condemned to a concentration camp in Potma, in the republic of Mordovia, where prisoners worked up to fourteen hours a day digging up the hard earth and loading it on a truck.

"What Olga remembered with most horror about the camp was a heartless female guard, who was even harsher than the climate and the work conditions." Irina pauses for a moment and then in a low voice she begins to tell that story. She speaks little by little, as if she were fulfilling an obligation, as if she were a child whom the teacher has called to the blackboard to explain a subject she doesn't want to touch. She identifies with her mother's experience. If her story is about her mother, it is also about herself, because, years later, Irina was also imprisoned in a forced labor camp in the same archipelago of camps where her mother had been confined. Irina's story comes from the experiences both women suffered.

"What my mother remembered as worst of all was the guard and the constant stifling heat of Mordovia. The heavy, white clouds floated slowly, very slowly over Potma. It seemed they were just circling over the same spot, too lazy to move on. The temperature could go up to one hundred and twenty degrees. In June, the sky would burn for long hours over the hard, dry land that the prisoners were expected to dig up.

"Olga was under the orders of the head of the work brigade, Buinaya, a skinny woman with a sharp nose, who enjoyed the confidence of the camp leaders and detested what she called 'the ladies from Moscow' with their 'white hands.' Winding up in Buinaya's brigade was the worst punishment.

"Olga, who had never done manual work, could barely lift the shovel when it was empty, much less when it was full. She didn't come near her quota, so her ration of food was reduced to a minimum. Buinaya hated Olga, among other reasons, because she was condemned to 'only' five years while Buinaya herself was in for ten. On top of it, Buinaya's two children were serving time in a camp in the north of Siberia.

"After Stalin's death and thanks to Pasternak's intervention, the authorities permitted Olga to leave the camp once they'd reviewed her case, but Buinaya died of tuberculosis before finishing her sentence in the same camp."

Irina's comment comes quickly: "Sometimes providence hands out its own form of justice."

"Olga didn't know how Boris was. Sometimes months went by without a letter from him. One day she found a postcard on the windowsill of the barracks. She looked at its contents: it was addressed to her, the handwriting was well known, yes, it was those flying cranes, those birds that Boris's writing resembled, carefree, like him, she thought. After that card, discovered by pure chance, she didn't receive another line for a long time. They were clearly not delivering her correspondence.

"To add to her misery, after the miscarriage that had been provoked by the authorities in Lubyanka, she bled copiously when she menstruated and before and after as well. More than once, she had asked for a day off during her period, but her request was turned down. One day in the fall, she had stayed in bed after washing her blood-soaked tunic, but they found her and forced her to work in the dripping tunic despite temperatures that were down to zero. Olga did everything they ordered for fear of being left without any news of home. Not knowing how her children and her mother were, in addition to Boris, was the worst punishment she could face."

{5}

Then came the strange night. When the prisoners' work was done that day, there was a deep reddish-purple sunset. It was beautiful, but it didn't augur well. Sunsets like that were usually followed the next day by unrelenting heat. The prisoners lined up to start their walk back to the barracks while the guards' German Shepherds looked at them with their tongues hanging out; like the prisoners, the dogs were thirsty and exhausted. All the women were searched by the guards to see if they had anything hidden under their work clothes.

"Later the moment they longed for came: they entered the barracks and collapsed on their beds without even the energy to take their boots off. They slept, perhaps even dreamed about their loved ones. Some even skipped the evening meal in the canteen in order to rest a little longer.

"Olga had no friends in the camp. She was too tired to try to make them. Most of the women around her were common prisoners, and she didn't know what to say to them. For most detainees, meeting other political prisoners shut in for the same reason—Article 58 of the penal code—meant the end of their solitude. For Olga, the solitude of the camp was infinite.

"After going to bed, Olga looked at herself in the little piece of glass that served as her mirror: the shard showed her the face of a woman whose features had become hard, her skin like parchment, her eyes red and her nose scaly. One of her incisors had broken in two. 'If I stay here another year, I'll become an old woman,' she sighed.

"In the middle of the night, they came for her. As she was being led out of the barracks, she didn't look at her comrades to avoid seeing the mocking expression on their faces as they watched her go. The guards used to come for women to be raped by the guards themselves or by their commanders. The prisoners were led out in the same way when they were going to denounce someone.

"When she was out in the street, Olga saw an enormous moon that lit up the whitewashed barracks. She also made out some tiny wildflowers beside the road. 'How beautiful all of this is, bathed in the moonlight,' she thought, in contrast to her stinking barracks, where you could hear insults and groans all night long. From the street, Olga made out a single lighted window in the inside of a room. She could see the light of a table lamp with a green shade and an open book. They had taken her to the house of the *kum*, the commander.

"A short, fat man with a red face told her that he had received an envelope. 'There's a long letter and a notebook of poetry. Sit down and read it here.'

"'Can't I take it to my barracks, even if it's just for a few days?'

"'That's not authorized. If you want to read what you've been sent, you'll have to do it here.'

"She spent the whole night reading: first the letter, again with the flying cranes, the free birds formed by Boris's handwriting. No, first she'd read the poems. She'd save the letter to the end.

You mean everything in my destiny,
Then came war, devastation,
And for a long, long time there was
No word of you, no trace.

She didn't know how long she had stayed there reading the poems in the notebook, but it must have been for hours. The letter was twelve pages long and filled with love. Olga never forgot his last words: 'Waiting for you constantly, my dearest one, your Boris, your Boria, writes all this to you.'

"This letter included his name and his surname, but despite that fact, even though it reached its destination, they did not give it to her, for whom it was intended. How many of these letters had been lost?

"The sky was turning pale, and the morning star had almost disappeared, when Olga left the commander's house and returned to her barracks. Luckily, her comrades were still sleeping so they couldn't look at her knowingly. She didn't go to bed, because reveille would soon sound. She looked at herself in the little piece of mirror and saw a shining face that was happy and young. That morning she didn't feel afraid of the work. She knew that the day would pass quickly and that she would be accompanied by the flying cranes."

{6}

Irina continues telling me the story of her mother:

"The month after Stalin's death in March 1953, an amnesty was announced for all the political prisoners who had been sentenced to less than five years. Olga was authorized to return from the Potma camp to Moscow and to live her life in freedom.

"She was exhausted when she got home. She entered her room and examined herself in the mirror on the wall. What she saw was a face and hands that had been hardened, but, following her in, I looked at the mirror and saw a thin, sun-tanned face that looked even younger. She was forty-one, but her split tooth gave her a lively air. At sixteen, I knew that my mother's good looks came from the wave of happiness that had washed over her on returning home to her children and her mother.

"That night, the whole family celebrated her return with great joy, but my mother's happiness did not last long. The next day she became depressed. She collapsed in a chair and said, in a voice I'd never heard, the voice of an old woman who is tired of life, 'You don't know what I've been through, what horrors I've seen and how many I've survived. I want nothing but peace. I don't even want to see Boris again.'

"I knew how to interpret my mother's desire for peace. Olga hadn't drawn away from Pasternak mentally and emotionally, but after what she had suffered in the camp, she didn't want to run the risk of having the authorities use her again in their efforts to punish the writer. They would do to her what they dared not do to him. In that moment, my mother only wanted to be left alone."

{7}

Pasternak felt guilty for the harsh punishment that had been inflicted on the woman he loved. That feeling made him withdraw from her. He didn't know how to face it, so he wasn't in a hurry to see her either. In her absence, he had missed her painfully, but at the same time it was easier not having to lead a double life, torn between wife and lover.

"However, soon after, Pasternak's wife, Zinaida, received a call from the writer Nikolai Aseev who informed her about Olga's return and told her that her husband used to take long walks with his lover. Aseev urged Zinaida to put her marriage in order. She tried, and after some very dramatic scenes, Pasternak promised that he would not see Olga again, but he couldn't bear staying away, so he began meeting her secretly. Again he became an essential part of Olga's life. Everything went back to the way it was before her arrest.

"All three suffered in that romantic triangle. Pasternak didn't have the willpower to do without Olga, who was life itself to him, but he couldn't make himself abandon Zinaida,

whom he loved 'like a mother loves her daughter,' as he himself said. 'I will live in this state of disorder until the end of my
days,' he wrote at the time. And that's what happened.

"Pasternak spent more and more time in his dacha in Peredelkino, a colony a few miles from Moscow. There writers
lived next to peasants who got around in carts in the summer
and in horse-drawn sleighs in the winter. On Pasternak's rec-
ommendation, Olga rented a room in a cabin in a neighboring
village, very close to the writer's dacha. They met there. They
worked together on the translations of Asian poets different
publishers had given to Olga so she could give them a poetic
form. They made every meal—even every tea—a celebration.
There they received their jolliest friends, people who were
not acceptable in Zinaida's house. I became a kind of adopted
daughter to the poet. Zinaida learned to look the other way
when her husband disappeared, and Olga got used to visits
from Boris that went on until late at night.

"The writer filled his poems and the pages of his novel
with the idyllic atmosphere that he enjoyed after his lover
came back from the Gulag.

"Olga took charge of part of Boris's work. She typed up
many of his poems, a number of which were included in the
last section of *Doctor Zhivago* as poems by Yuri Zhivago, and
she learned them by heart. She did it so they would help her
through the hard times she felt were bound to return, but also
so they would keep her company in the good times. Olga
walked through the streets of Moscow or arranged her room
in Peredelkino and, when she wasn't singing, she recited in a
low voice, from memory, the long poem 'Autumn':

I've let the family go its ways,
All those close to me have long dispersed,
And the usual solitude
Fills all of nature and my heart.

And so I am here with you in the cabin,
In the unpeopled and deserted forest.
The paths and trails, as in a song,
Are half submerged in undergrowth.

Now the log walls gaze in sorrow
At us alone. We never promised
To take the obstacles, if we perish,
We shall do it openly.

We sit down at one, get up at three,
I with a book, you with your sewing,
And at dawn we won't have noticed
How at some point we stopped kissing."

{8}

Pasternak continued working on his novel. Once he had finally finished it, however, no publisher in the Soviet Union had the nerve to bring it out. In addition, all the editors and literary reviews knew that, even if they took the risk of including it in their catalog, the censors would not authorize its publication, so it became clear that *Doctor Zhivago* would not be coming out in the USSR in spite of the supposed thaw in cultural life under Khrushchev.

On a sunny day at the end of May, two men took the commuter train in Moscow and traveled to Peredelkino. One of them was a Russian, Vladlen Vladimirsky, the other was Sergio D'Angelo, an emissary from Feltrinelli, an Italian publishing house. When the two of them reached Pasternak's house, he stopped working in his vegetable garden and hurried to meet them. The three men sat on benches in the garden surrounded by flowering lilacs that perfumed the air. Pasternak took a liking to his Italian visitor. He couldn't stop talking about his visits to Venice and Florence when he was a student.

D'Angelo turned the conversation to the subject of Pasternak's work. The writer confessed with deep sadness that he had recently finished his novel, the great work of his life, but that not a single Soviet editor had shown any interest. D'Angelo was waiting for that moment. He offered to publish the novel in Italy with Feltrinelli. The writer liked the idea. D'Angelo promised, moreover, that the Italian editor, Giangiacomo Feltrinelli, would sell the rights to other countries, especially to France and Great Britain. Pasternak felt as though a dream had come true, and the Italian emissary could read this reaction in his face. The writer went up to his office on the second floor of the dacha and came back with the manuscript of the novel, which was more than four hundred pages long typed in single space. D'Angelo cast a glance at the fat sheaf of papers and hid it quickly in his briefcase. When they said their goodbyes, Pasternak shook the Italian's hand and commented with an ironic smile, "You are invited to my execution."

{9}

Soon after that meeting, the emissary smuggled the manuscript to Milan, and the Italian editor announced its imminent publication. In the two years that followed, *Zhivago* was published in twenty-four languages. Pasternak was so overwhelmed by letters from publishers in countries throughout the world that he had to ask Olga for help. She became his secretary and literary agent.

Zhivago was read all over the world. In 1958, Pasternak won the Nobel Prize for literature. In his interviews with the Western press, the writer said that very few Russians shared his delight over the prize. In the end, the following message went out to the West: "Under pressure from the Soviet authorities, who have not given the sick writer a moment of peace, Pasternak has been forced to renounce the most prestigious literary prize in the world."

Even after his renunciation, the attacks on Pasternak did not let up. They were constant.

But there was another, essential reason for Pasternak's renunciation, of which the Western press was unaware: Olga.

{10}

Irina insists that he gave up the prize because of Olga. Pasternak's first born son, Evgeni, told me something very similar in 2012 before his death: "Pasternak was afraid that in order to take revenge on him for having published *Doctor Zhivago* abroad, the state would persecute his lover Olga, who was much more vulnerable."

"The state would take revenge?" I asked.

"In this respect, the Soviet state may have been different from other dictatorships and totalitarian governments. It was vengeful, even capricious," Evgeni maintained.

A few years later, the writer Svetlana Alexievich agreed with him: "The KGB often took revenge on Russian intellectuals. What it did to Pasternak is one example," she told me in a private talk.

{11}

E veryone remembers some moment of their life as special," Irina says, and her smile shines in the dim light of the kitchen. "Mine is without doubt the celebration of New Year's Eve in 1959 and the arrival of 1960. There were four of us: my mother, Pasternak, Georges Nivat—my French boyfriend, who was studying in Moscow—and I. Boris's handsome face, illuminated by the candles that we had put on the Christmas tree and the table, looked almost as though it had been sculpted out of marble. And yet, in the golden light, I suddenly felt that his expression was that of a man who was not long for this world. I told myself that my impression was due to the weak light of the candles that hollowed out the angles of his face as though it were a Cubist painting.

"Georges Nivat opened the first bottle of French champagne, and we toasted the special new year that was just starting. Georges and I were going to get married and move to Paris. Pasternak was planning to premiere a new play that he had just finished. 'Happy New Year! A new year and a new life!' we toasted. Later Olga served roast chicken. The glasses of champagne sparkled as we celebrated the arrival of a year that would be even happier than the old one. We exchanged our presents enthusiastically. The present Georges gave Pasternak, an engraving of the four ages of man, was the least successful. Boris gave it a quick look and then rolled it up as if it reminded him of something disagreeable. Once again, I had, just briefly, the strange sensation that had seized me at the beginning of the evening. But I forgot about it when we began to sing Christmas carols. Georges remembered some French ones, and Olga sang traditional Russian songs.

"At eleven o'clock, Pasternak got up to go back home, where his other family, along with their guests, and another supper were waiting for him. Aware of his difficulty walking, the three of us accompanied him up to the last bend before he reached his house."

{12}

The year got off to a grand start. In my fourth year at the University of Moscow, I was preparing for my exams, and Georges, who was a student at the Lumumba University for foreigners, was working on his dissertation. We were living in a little country house with a steep roof that was almost buried under the snow. My mother came from Moscow very often and stayed with us.

"We were waiting impatiently for the sun to come out, so we could go skiing. When it did, Georges and I took off over the plain and then reached the rolling white landscape. The air was so cold and crisp that it left us breathless. We were heading toward the woods. We skied up hills and then down, whooping like children. Our hands and feet were freezing, but we kept on going through the woods, which we knew inside and out: the clearings, the hills, and the tender young firs that were almost the same color as the snow that covered them. Sometimes we really went a long way, up to twenty kilometers. We were so fascinated by that shining, marvelous world that we lost track of the time, lost ourselves, sank into the high, virgin snow and the snowbanks. When we were frozen, tired, and hungry, we'd race back across the vast windswept plain until we reached our snow-covered house. After four o'clock, the violet-colored twilight came down fast.

"Laughing, we rushed into the house, lit the stove as fast as we could and started cooking. Afterwards, we studied a little, but more than anything we waited for somebody...who always wound up coming.

"Around eight, while the snowflakes twirled in the darkness, we could hear steps at the front door. Georges and I raced to greet the guest who came every night with absolute regularity, even though he knew that Olga might not be there. He liked seeing that, in the shadows, amid the snow and the winds, there was a lighted window that shone just for him. On the other side of the window, people were waiting for his arrival.

"Boris was covered with snow. Georges helped him take off his heavy fur coat and hung it by the fire while Boris asked, 'Is Olga here?' or 'Has Mama come?' Sometimes, if she were there, he'd exclaim joyfully, 'Hi, Microphone! How are you? Give my regards to the listeners!' He was, of course, talking about the devices that the KGB installed in our place to record our conversations.

"Even if my mother wasn't there, I would invite Boris to have a glass of the champagne that Georges had brought from France. When our provisions ran out, he'd buy it in the special stores for foreigners, the *Beryozka* shops, in Moscow. 'I've come for just a few minutes,' Boris would say, but later we'd wind up drinking the whole bottle."

{13}

One afternoon that winter, they took Pasternak for an interrogation in the headquarters of the KGB in Moscow because of a poem entitled 'Nobel Prize.' In it, the author expresses his surprise that the authorities treated him like an evildoer when the only crime he had committed was showing the world, in *Doctor Zhivago*, the beauty of his country. My mother asked for permission to be present at the interrogation because of Pasternak's fragile state, and she obtained it.

"During the preceding weeks, Olga had noticed that Boris tired easily when they were searching for ways to turn the literal translations they had of Georgian, Armenian, and Chinese poetry into poetic form in Russian. Moreover, he tired quickly when he walked, much more so than a few months earlier. Although Boris avoided the subject of his health and made a point of acting like a strong, robust man, my mother knew there were reasons to worry.

"When the interrogation ended, the couple walked down the staircase of the KGB building. Boris was furious: 'Did you see? They're not like people. They don't have the slightest human feeling. Within these horrible walls, they all become automatons!'

"I met them downstairs, in the waiting room, because they had denied me permission to be present at the interview. Afterwards, in the official, chauffeur-driven car that took us to Peredelkino, I recited some fragments of Pasternak's poem 'Evil Days' in *Zhivago*:

> *And the dark powers of the Temple let scoundrels*
> *Hand him to the scum for judgment,*
> *And with the same ardor as they praised him*
> *Earlier they cursed now.*

> *The crowd from the lot next door*
> *Peered in through the gates,*
> *Jostling and shoving each other*
> *As they waited for the outcome.*

"We returned to Peredelkino and accompanied Pasternak to his house. He had turned down our invitation to have tea with us, because he didn't feel well. We all noticed the change in him, my mother more than anyone."

Irina has a sip of tea, and, trying to avoid the sense of sorrow, she continues with a mischievous smile: "Then the huge, black, official car that had brought us there, the famous 'crow,' got stuck in the mud. The whole town came out to enjoy the spectacle: the official driver, dressed in an impeccably ironed dark suit and a tie, got out and pushed the shining 'crow,' a symbol of Soviet power, that had made up its mind not to move. The impeccable chauffeur also sank into the mud, up to his knees, from so much pushing, but … the car didn't budge!"

Irina finally stops laughing and says that the next day when Pasternak and Georges, each holding a glass of champagne, heard the story, they just cracked up.

{14}

After a year of the constant persecution that followed the Nobel Prize and the publication of *Doctor Zhivago* abroad, all made worse by his fears for Olga, Pasternak's health deteriorated dramatically. He had lung cancer. At first, he kept up his custom of going to see Olga every day even though she advised him to stay home when it was cold. Then he stopped visiting her, but he wrote affectionate letters instead. Later on, he stopped writing, and his family confirmed that he was so weak he couldn't even sit up.

"On May 30, 1960, Pasternak died at the age of seventy," says Irina, and continues:

"On June 2, before attending the funeral which, as Pasternak wished, was to be held at the Peredelkino cemetery, hundreds of readers, artists, and intellectuals showed up at his house to pay their tributes. They brought bunches of flowers for his coffin. Maria Yudina and Sviatoslav Richter played the piano in the next room. Yudina played Mozart; Richter, Chopin. Then, to show it was time to set off for the cemetery, Richter played Chopin's *Funeral March.* Thousands of people congregated in the cemetery. After the official address, which referred to Pasternak as a brilliant translator and made no reference to *Doctor Zhivago,* a young man who was not on the program stood up. He described *Doctor Zhivago* as the greatest novel of the post-revolutionary era and decried the fact that in the writer's own country the publication of that literary treasure had never been authorized.

"My mother, who had not seen Pasternak for a long time, had gone to his house to say good-bye. She made an effort to be brave, but in the end, she broke down and started weeping. During almost the entire service, she stayed with Georges and me, sitting in the garden at the Pasternak house, unable to stand up or to talk to anyone. At the last, Georges and I helped her go to the cemetery. She wanted to keep her suffering to herself, but when she saw Boris in the coffin beside the open tomb, she burst into tears.

"She was thinking about the last months, when he was too sick to get out of bed. She had found out that for days Boris had expressed his desire to die peacefully, but the doctors kept waking him up with injections that gave him an artificial life. The dying man would tell his children, 'I am tired of standing up for human talent, real talent that's playful and free. Around me, around us, all I see is banality and vulgarity. The world will sink in this mud.'

"Sitting on her bench, my mother thought about the family's refusal to let her see Boris. They claimed that he did not want to see her. Olga knew how to interpret that: Boris wanted his lover to remember him always as strong and handsome. He was ashamed for her to see him as fragile and downcast, with his face dry and yellowish like parchment, his eyes wet and his limbs slack. But to leave her without even saying good-bye. . . .

"At the same time, she realized she would find herself in an even weaker position in relation to Soviet power than she had been during his life. She felt uneasy and anguished, not just over the loss of the man who had filled her life for fifteen years but over the loss of his protection. Now she would be at the mercy of the KGB.

"She thought about *Doctor Zhivago*, the novel that spoke about the two of them and that was so compelling that my mother had always seen their lives as predestined by the logic of the plot. She could picture the novel's end: Yuri Zhivago abandoning Lara and her daughter Katia like a coward, leaving Lara, who is pregnant with his child, in the hands of Victor Komarovsky, a man who once seduced her and whom she despises; Zhivago's conviction that such an action is necessary for the good of Lara and Katia, turning his head away from his lover's pregnancy. Just like Pasternak, my mother thought, who had not known what to do with her and her daughter.

Like his character, he let things take their course, without re-sisting, without making decisions.

"And with a shiver, she remembered the last words of the novel, just before the epilogue, the words that spoke of Lara, Larisa, her alter ego: 'Larissa Fyodorovna left home and did not return. Apparently, they arrested her in the street. She died or dis-appeared who knows where, forgotten under a number without a name on a list that was lost, in one of those miserable concen-tration camps in the north for common criminals or for women.'

"My mother had a presentiment about her future, and a chill ran down her spine.

"Among the thousands of people who attended the fu-neral, she was one of the last to take her leave of the body before they covered the coffin and buried it under the ground. She turned her face, bathed in tears, toward the wind that was much more noticeable in the elevated cemetery than under the gilded cupolas of the little white church in the village. Faintly she heard some young voices reciting the poem that, years ago, he had composed for her.

I'm no more, but you're still alive,
And the wind, complaining, weeping,
Sways the forest and the dacha. . . ."

{15}

While Olga was saying good-bye to Boris, the Central Committee of the Communist Party of the USSR was preparing an announcement intended for the Union of Soviet Writers, warning them to be vigilant about students of literature, because 'some of them are poisoned by the harmful ideas of the opposition and will try to convert Pasternak into a great writer who was misunderstood by his epoch.'"

{16}

The day after the funeral, KGB agents came to the apartment on Potapovsky Street, where Olga was living with us, her son and daughter. They took practically everything: the manuscripts, including the second part of *Doctor Zhivago*, which Pasternak had given Olga, and *The Blind Beauty*, the play that was his last work, a manuscript he had also given to my mother, as well as the letters they had written to each other and even some of our furniture. Olga tried to seize the manuscript from their hands, but the secret police threatened her coldly: 'Next time we'll set up an appointment for you at the institution, where the conversations tend to be much more traumatic than in a private apartment.'

"From that day on, every time my mother traveled to Peredelkino, she was awaited by a forest of trees that moved. The bushes followed her when she returned to her home and they crept along behind her when she went back to the train station. It was like the forest in *Macbeth*, but this time hiding KGB agents."

{17}

After Pasternak's death, the KGB did not just feed on Olga, but on Irina and Georges Nivat as well. From my conversations with both of them, I deduced what had happened.

Georges and Irina were planning to get married in Moscow before moving to Paris, but before the wedding Georges got sick. No one knew what he had. It was a mystery. He was covered from head to toe in blisters and had a high fever. He was hospitalized. It turned out that he was suffering from an extremely contagious infectious disease.

"It didn't happen by chance," Irina insisted. "In our country undesirable people tend to come down with all sorts of mysterious illnesses."

The young man got better in the hospital. He was well enough to walk, but the doctors did not release him. He asked them to let him leave even if it was only for a couple of hours, but his requests were refused. The hospital authorities were inflexible. A guard was posted behind the door of his room day and night. Georges decided to make an escape through a first-floor window which was not guarded. Irina took him a shirt, a pair of jeans, and some track shoes. The two young people went off to request a wedding date. They were assigned August 8.

Georges was finally free from the hospital, but immediately encountered another obstacle: the Soviet authorities had not renewed his visa even though the French ambassador had presented a request to Khrushchev himself. On August 6, two days before the wedding, KGB agents showed up in Georges's room at the dormitory. They took him to the airport and forced him onto the last plane that was leaving Moscow for Helsinki.

Georges Nivat is now a highly regarded specialist in Russian literature and a translator of Russian classics. When I asked him about being poisoned by the Soviet authorities in Moscow, he told me: "I write books and give interviews, but up until now I have never referred to that period in my life. The truth is that I nearly died twice from mysterious illnesses that were very painful and led to long stays in the hospital, but that is something I prefer not to discuss."

{18}

After Pasternak's death, my mother was totally disconsolate. She was also paralyzed with fear. She didn't know when the KGB agents would return, but she was sure it would be soon. To have something else to think about, she decided to move her old armoire from Moscow to her little house in the country. The day she planned to move it, August 16, 1960 (exactly ten days after my fiancé was expelled from the country), she peered into my room. I was in bed, sick.

"'Don't get up, darling; take care of yourself. I'll be back at about five.'

"She didn't come back. In her house in Peredelkino, she was drinking tea with her mother and her mother's second husband when KGB agents burst into the garden. 'I suppose you were expecting us, weren't you?' one of them said, looking pleased with himself. 'You must have realized that your anti-Soviet activities wouldn't go unpunished, right?' Then they arrested her and took her off to prison.

"During the eighteen months before Pasternak's death, the KGB had noticed different foreigners bringing in money for the writer. By selling the rights to *Zhivago* to dozens of publishers all over the world, Pasternak had become a rich man. He had authorized Feltrinelli to give a hundred thousand dollars of his royalties to D'Angelo to convert into rubles and carry to Moscow. Feltrinelli transferred the money from an account set up in a tax haven in Lichtenstein to D'Angelo, who changed it into rubles. 'My love, what do you think we should do with all this money?' Pasternak asked Olga once D'Angelo had left them alone with his piles of rubles. Olga looked around her. 'Let's hide it in that suitcase,' she said, gesturing toward an old bag in a corner. And that's what they did.

"Another time, an Italian woman called Pasternak at Olga's house, which was certainly bugged, and said that she wanted to give him a package of books. Olga could not move, because she had strained a tendon, and Pasternak did not want to take the risk of meeting up with an unknown foreign woman, so I was the one who met her. When Pasternak opened the briefcase the woman had given me, we saw that it was full of Soviet bills, lined up in little piles that were wrapped in fine paper."

{19}

That money from the royalties gave the Soviet state an excuse to turn my mother and me into scapegoats for the entire *Zhivago* affair. After Pasternak's death, I got sicker and sicker. Ironically, I only got better when they took me to Lubyanka. Like my French fiancé, I had also been poisoned by the Soviet authorities.

"It was in Lubyanka that I found my mother again, four months after we were arrested. That's when we began to suspect that those mysterious ailments originated in the KGB labs, with their sophisticated poisons.

"My mother had always taken pride in her appearance. Now her eyes were red; she was so thin she looked sick, and her dress was not even buttoned up right. The change in her was made very clear by the harsh light of a bare bulb that was never turned off.

"Then in November 1960, seven years after Stalin's death, when many people believed that the dictator's arbitrary arrests were a thing of the past and the concentration camps had been closed for good, our case went to trial. The verdict was pronounced behind closed doors; they didn't even let my little brother attend. A secret tribunal decreed a harsh sentence, condemning both of us to the expropriation of our goods, along with eight years of prison and forced labor for my mother and three for me. We were accused of the unlawful use of foreign currency (the money that my mother had received from the publication in the West of *Doctor Zhivago*, which Pasternak had given her; it was, of course, a pretext).

"Afterwards they transferred us to the Lefortovo prison and assigned us to separate cells. I was twenty-two, my mother forty-eight. We both preferred this building, which was luminous compared to Lubyanka. It had high ceilings and was constructed in the czarist era. It also offered a bathroom that was relatively accessible. I used to recite the poems I could remember to my cellmates."

{20}

At the end of January, after two and a half months in prison, they summoned them for the trip to the work camp. It was thirty degrees below zero when they put them on the train. No one told them where they were going. The car was freezing, and they trembled with cold in the company of other women prisoners: thieves, lesbians, vagabonds, and six nuns. "Where are they taking us?" Irina's mother asked their travel companions, especially the younger ones who had not yet sunk into a permanently sullen state. At the first stop, Irina's mother offered some cigarettes to a boy through the bars on the window to find out where they were going. "To the work camp in Tayshet," he told her when he had asked someone. "You have a long way to go."

Tayshet, Tayshet... Irina remembered what she had learned in school: Tayshet was a little city in the Irkutsk region of Siberia.

It was nighttime when, after days and days of traveling, the train entered a station. Because of the train's involved maneuvers, the women deduced that it was a large city. One could read the name on the signs: Sverdlovsk. "Does anybody know what this city was called before the arrival of the Antichrist?" one of the nuns asked worriedly as she got off.

"Yekaterinburg, that's what it was called before the Anti-christ," Irina told the nuns.

Mother Natalia bowed and said, "Sisters, welcome to one of the capitals of the realm, Yekaterinburg."

The prisoners trembled in the nighttime cold—it was thirty degrees below zero—while the guards went through folders that were filled with documents. They called each prisoner by her full name, just as they would twice a day for years in the Gulag. To take her mind off things, Irina raised her head and looked up at the Siberian sky, so different from the sky above Moscow. Here the constellations stood out clearly in the darkness, assuming extraordinary forms.

{21}

Hurry up! Let's go! Step on it!'
"We grabbed our bundles and tried to drag them across the snow. But after almost a month of traveling in the worst conditions, my mother and I were tired and frozen, and we lagged behind. The head of the guards, a common pris-oner, hurled insults at us. My mother could not bear it.

"'Help us! Please! My daughter has been sick, and she's not well yet. And now you're laughing at us. It's the last thing we need!'

"'You've got a lot of nerve! You've committed a crime, and this is the punishment you deserve. And if somebody is sick, well, that's just part of the punishment!'

"'You lout!' screamed Olga, desperate now. 'Nobody knows why we're here. We aren't guilty of anything. Have you heard about Pasternak? About his novel *Doctor Zhivago*? About his protagonist, Lara?'

"'Mama, stop, please!' I tried to calm her. 'To hell with our bags. We'll leave them here, and that's it. But don't sink to the level of these....'

"'I've had enough of you!' the guard shouted at my mother. 'When we get to the camp, I'll have them shut you up in solitary!'

"After walking and walking, when we were on the point of collapse and were thinking about just falling into the high piles of virgin snow, we made out a black transport vehicle in the distance that would move the prisoners. The guards separated my mother from the others and made her sit in the back of the car, in a tiny, barred cubicle. They threw our bundles inside, even the nuns' toasted bread. The nuns began to sing their luminous songs about Christ in a low voice. I asked one of them if they believed they were going to die soon and were preparing for their end. One of them, who was sitting next to me, whispered in my ear that the crucifixion would be the next day.

"At some point, we had to get out of the vehicle and walk through the woods. This time a horse carried our bundles. For the rest of my life I have trembled every time I remember that long walk over the snow, at night, with the temperature dropping lower and lower. But I also remember the beauty of the night, which was quiet and silvery with a full moon that projected the pale blue shadows of the short pines and the deep blue tones of the tall Siberian fir trees over the white snow. Yet, although the land was beautiful, the forest seemed ominous.

"While we were walking, my mother was worrying about the future. How were we going to survive? I was wearing a short, thin overcoat, with stylish sleeves that did not come down to my wrists. Until now, I had worn that lightweight coat only for special occasions, but the authorities had not allowed me to take my fur coat to the camp. How could we tolerate the hard work that awaited us? It would surely involve cutting down trees and laying train tracks.

"I trembled even though I was walking fast, and my bones were chilled from the cold. Suddenly, as if in a fairy tale, I made out lights that seemed to draw nearer as the human convoy advanced. The lights came from a cowshed, where we spent that night. The next day we had to reach the Tayshet camp. There we were expected to clear paths in the frozen snow.

"If the temperature dropped lower than thirty-five degrees below zero, we didn't have to go out to work. Every morning we looked at the thermometer that hung on a corner outside with great anxiety: 'Maybe we'll be lucky today!'

"I had had no news of my fiancé, Georges. Would my dream of marrying him and living in Paris ever be realized? My mother knew that the Soviet Ministry of Internal Affairs would never allow that wish to come true, but she did not spoil my happy illusion. It helped me survive.

"Many prisoners in the camp were given a nickname; they wound up calling my mother and me 'The Pasternakettes.'"

{22}

At the end of a month, they sent the two of us from Siberia to the work camp intended for the most serious political cases. It was in Potma, in the republic of Mordovia. That's exactly where my mother had been confined a decade earlier. We had to repeat the awful trip we had taken just a month before, but now in the opposite direction, while we wondered what had brought on this decision. We concluded that it could only be the sadism of the Ministry of Internal Affairs.

"My mother was nearly fifty, a difficult age for a woman, and she had a particularly hard time with it. She was convinced that she couldn't bear forced labor in that camp for the second time, and she tried to commit suicide.

"They saved her life, but when she left the Gulag, she was broken. She would never again be that strong, happy, and carefree woman who had inspired Pasternak for the character of Lara."

Irina remains quiet for a time when I ask her about the working conditions in Potma. Finally, she says, "I described them in detail when I told my mother's story. Very little had changed from that time. But, yes, there was a small change: we didn't have to fulfill a quota. The rest was the same. What I remember most clearly is the winter, its beauty and the cold that I felt intensely, the icy wind that seemed to cut through our bones. Another change implemented after Stalin's death was that the prisoners did not have to work if the temperature fell below a certain temperature: in Siberia, minus thirty-five degrees, but in Mordovia, twenty-five below zero was the cut-off point. And in this camp there was a sense of camaraderie. I still have friends, even today, that I made there. Without these friends, many of us in the Gulag would have been lost or even dead. Besides that, I was lucky in always having my mother by my side."

But something important happened in the Gulag, something that changed Irina's life entirely. She met a prisoner from the men's camp, a poet and translator of French poetry. Like her mother and Pasternak two decades before, Irina communicated with her friend through poetry. Vadim Kozovoy left his poems under a brick in the wall that separated the two camps. Irina picked them up and, in their place, left poems by Pasternak that she had written in pencil on little scraps of paper. When they had gotten to know each other through the poems, Vadim gave Irina his diary to read. She shows it to me. The entries are long and written in a minuscule handwriting to take advantage of all the space in the notebook, since any kind of paper was very hard to come by in the camps.

Like many survivors of the Gulag who chose their partners from among other survivors because only the survivors could really understand what it meant to overcome that kind of experience, Irina married the man who knew how to light up her days in the camp with poetry.

"He turned out to be a difficult person. The Gulag marked him for life. But with each other, we felt understood. The most important thing in life is to feel understood," she concludes.

{23}

We are saying good-bye. While I'm putting on my overcoat, hat, and muffler, I remember to ask about her French fiancé. Irina tells me that when Georges received the letter saying she was marrying another man, he volunteered to do his military service in Algiers, where he was wounded in an ambush.

"For twelve years Georges tried unsuccessfully to get a visa for the USSR," Irina tells me. "When they finally allowed him in, he went directly to see me, and he made friends with my husband, the poet Kozovoy."

At the end of the 1960s, although it was before the beginning of perestroika in 1985, Kozovoy managed to move to Paris with his son who needed specialized medical attention. Irina got there with their young son years later. The couple remained in Paris, leaving Olga behind although Irina visited her often. All of this became much easier once perestroika began. Olga wrote a memoir about her life with Pasternak, *Hostage of Eternity* (1978), which came out in several languages. She died in 1995. Irina taught Russian at the Sorbonne and published two memoirs. Vadim Kozovoy kept on writing poetry. The literary critic Maurice Blanchot wrote about him, and the poet and translator Michel Deguy translated his work into French. He kept up a correspondence with the poet René Char and was a friend of Henri Michaux, artist and poet. He also translated the great contemporary French poets into Russian. He died in 1999 at seventy-one.

"He died translating poetry," Irina explains to me. "Poetry was his whole life. He was translating *Les Illuminations* by Rimbaud—*je me trouvai néanmoins chez ma dame, en gros oiseau gris bleu s'essorant vers les moulures du plafond*—when he had a heart attack."

After democracy was established in Russia, Irina visited her homeland more often until she wound up spending long periods there, dividing her time between Paris and Moscow. However, in recent years, she has avoided Putin's Russia, finding it inhospitable and dangerous.

When I leave Irina's house in Paris and walk through the nocturnal, autumnal city, her words resound in my head: "The most important thing in life is to feel understood."

BIBLIOGRAPHY

Akhmatova, Anna, *The Complete Poems of Anna Akhmatova*. Translated by Judith Hemschemeyer. Zephyr Press, Boston, 1990.

Amis, Martin, *House of Meetings*. Alfred Knopf, New York, 2007.

Applebaum, Ann, *Gulag. A History*. Random House, New York, 2003.

Berlin, Isaiah, *Letters 1928–1946*. Edited by Henry Hardy. Cambridge University Press, 2004.

Buber-Neumann, Margarete, *Under Two Dictators: Prisoner of Stalin and Hitler*. Translated by Edward Fitgerald. Penguin Books, London 2008.

Cohen, Stephen, *The Victims Return: Survivors of the Gulag After Stalin*. Publishing Works, Exeter 2010.

Chamberdji, Valentina, *Lina Prokófiev. Una española en el gulag*. Siglo XXI de España Editores, Madrid 2009.

Courtois, Stéphane, ed., *The Black Book of Communism: Crimes, Terror, Repression*. Harvard University Press, 2009.

Efron, Ariadna, *Chronique d'un goulag ordinaire*. Phébus, Paris, 2005.

Efron, Ariadna, *Pisma iz ssylki (1948–1957) Borisu Pasternaku*. YMCA Press, Paris, 1982.

Emelyanova, Irina, *Legendy Potapovskogo pereulka*. Ellis Lak, Moscow, 1997.

Emelyanova, Irina, *Pasternak i Ivinskaya*. Vagrius, Moscow, 2006.

Figes, Orlando, *Just Send Me Word*. Penguin, New York, London, 2012.

Ginzburg, Evgenia, *Krutoi marsbrut*. Possev-USA, New York, 1985.

Ginzburg, Evgenia, *Journey into the Whirlwind*. Translated by Paul Stevenson and Max Hayward, New York, 1967.

Gumilyov, Lev, *Iz istorii Evrazii*. Iskusstvo, Moscow, 1993.

Iyevleva, Valentina, *Neprichesannaya zhizn*. Vozvrashchenie, Moscow, 1994.

Ivinskaya, Olga, *V plenu vremeni. Gody s Borisom Pasternakom*. Librairie Arthème Fayard, Paris, 1978.

Kersnovskaya, Evfrosinia, *The price of a Human Being/Skolko stoit chelovek*. ROSSPEN, Moscow, 2006.

Markova, Elena, *Vorkutinskie Zametki Katorzhanki E-105*. Syktyvkar, Komi, 2006.

Markova, Elena, *Zhili-byli v XX veke*. Syktyvkar, Komi, 2006.

Matthews, Owen, *Stalin's Children: Three Generations of Love, War, and Survival*. Walker & Co, New York, 2008.

Miller, Andrew, *The Lost Spy*. Norton & Company, New York, London, 2008.

Okunevskaya, Tatiana, *Tatyanin den*. Vagrius, Moscow, 2005.

Rossi, Jacques, *The Gulag Handbook*. Paragonhouse, New York, 1989.

Sepetys, Ruta, *Between Shades of Gray*. Penguin, New York, 2011.

Serrano, Secundino, *Españoles en el gulag: republicanos bajo el estalinismo*. Península, Barcelona, 2011.

Solzhenitsyn, Alexander, *The Gulag Archipelago*, 3 volumes. New York, 1973.

Solzhenitsyn, Alexander, *One Day in the Life of Ivan Denisovich.* Translated by Ralph Parker. New American Library, Penguin USA, New York, 2009.

Shalamov, Varlam, *Kolyma Stories.* Translated by Donald Rayfield. New York Review of Books, New York, 2018.

Shapovalov, Veronica, ed. and trans., *Remembering the Darkness: Women in Soviet Prisons.* Rowman & Littlefield Publishers, Lanham, Boulder, New York, Oxford, 2001.

Shentalinsky, Vitaly, *The KGB Literary Archives.* Harvill Press, London, 1993.

Štajner, Karlo, *7,000 Days in Siberia.* Farrar, Straus and Giroux, New York, 1988.

Thubron, Colin, *In Siberia.* HarperCollins, New York, 1999.

Tobien, Karl, *Dancing Under the Red Star: The Extraordinary Story of Margaret Werner, the Only American Woman to Survive Stalin's Gulag.* Waterbrook Press, Colorado Springs, 2006.

Vesyolaya, Zayara, *7-35. Vospominania o tyurme i ssylke.* Vozvrashchenie, Moscow, 2006.

Vilensky, Semyon, et al., *Deti Gulaga: 1918–1956.* Vozvrashchenie, Moscow, 2002.

Vilensky, Semyon, ed., *Dodnes tyagoteet.* Vozvrashchenie, Moscow, 2004.

Vilensky, Semyon, ed., *Poezia uznikov gulaga. Antologia.* Mezhdunarodnyi Fond "Demokratia," Moscow, 2005.

Vilensky, Semyon, *Till My Tale Is Told.* Indiana University Press, Bloomington, 1999.

MONIKA ZGUSTOVA is an award-winning author whose works have been published in ten languages. She was born in Prague and studied comparative literature at the University of Illinois and the University of Chicago. She then moved to Barcelona, where she writes for *El País*, *The Nation*, and *CounterPunch*, among others. As a translator of Czech and Russian literature into Spanish and Catalan—including the writing of Havel, Kundera, Hrabal, Hašek, Dostoyevsky, Akhmatova, Tsvetaeva, and Babel—Zgustova is credited with bringing major twentieth-century writers to Spain.

JULIE JONES is Professor Emeritus of Spanish at the University of New Orleans. She has published widely on the Latin American writers of the "Boom," with a focus on Luis Buñuel's work in numerous articles for such journals as *Cineaste* and *Cinema Journal*.